THE
MEANING
OF
SUFFERING

*Margaret Story
from Jo-Anne Aldred*

THE MEANING OF SUFFERING

RALPH W. SOCKMAN

WOMAN'S DIVISION OF CHRISTIAN SERVICE
BOARD OF MISSIONS, THE METHODIST CHURCH

To

BISHOP HERBERT WELCH

*The President of My College
for Four Years,
The Pattern of My Pulpit
for Forty Years
A Noble Exemplar of Christian Living
for Almost a Century*

SUPPLEMENTARY MATERIALS
For the Study of
THE MEANING OF SUFFERING

These materials may be ordered from Literature Headquarters, Woman's Division of Christian Service, 7820 Reading Road, Cincinnati 37, Ohio.

    GUIDE on THE MEANING OF SUFFERING by Leila Bagley Rumble. 35 cents.

    PLAYLET, *Stretch Forth Thine Hand* by Betsy Stockton Wolfe. 35 cents.

    PRAYER CALENDAR, *The Current Prayer Calendar*. An Itinerary of Prayer. (Methodist missionaries, deaconesses, and commissioned workers are listed on their birthdays and in an alphabetical name and address list. Mission work in the United States and around the world is listed geographically and alphabetically. Maps.) 60 cents; 3 for $1.50.

LEAFLETS:

    Say a Prayer With Me Before You Go, by Russell L. Dicks. 3 cents.

    Who Would Valiant Be, by Maude White Hardie. 2 cents.

    Medical Work, by Mrs. E. U. Robinson. Department of Work in Home Fields, Woman's Division of Christian Service. Free.

    Opening New Windows. (A pictorial leaflet about children's homes of the Woman's Division of Christian Service.) Free.

    When You Visit the Sick, by Marietta Mansfield. Free.

    The Will of God, by Leslie Weatherhead. 50 cents.

PRAYER CARD:

    Let Me Remember, by Maude White Hardie. 2 cents.

Contents

INTRODUCTION ix

Chapter

I   THE SOURCES OF SUFFERING 1
   Sources of Suffering We Can Understand . 1
     Suffering Due to Sin 1
     Suffering Due to Individual Guilt 3
     Suffering Due to Collective Guilt 5
     Collective Suffering 6
     Suffering Caused by Our Enemies 7
     Suffering Due to Mistakes 8
   Sources of Suffering We Do Not Understand 10
     Chance 10
     Accidents 12
     Acts of God 13
   Suggestions for Further Thought 16

II THE PAIN OF LIVING—HOW TO FACE IT .. 20
   Facing the Unforeseeable 20
   Misunderstanding 24
   Disappointment 27
   Anxiety 32
   Persecution 37

III PHYSICAL AND MENTAL ILLNESS 41
   Pain 41
   Disability 45
   Mental Illness 49
   Faith and Healing 56

Chapter

IV THE VALUES OF SUFFERING 66
    Discipline 66
    Growth 70
    Resourcefulness 78
    Understanding 83
    Assurance 86
    Helpfulness 89

V DEATH 93
    How to Face One's Own Death 93
    How to Accept the Death of a Loved One 101
    How to Help Those Who Are Bereaved .. 108
    The Art of Leaving 110

VI THE FELLOWSHIP OF SUFFERING 114
    Must the Good Pay for the Bad? 114
    Life's Deepest Law 120
    Troubles We Can Avoid 124
    Troubles We Cannot Avoid 126
    Troubles We Must Not Avoid 129
    The Spirit and Power of Compassion 131

NOTES 137

BOOKS RELATED TO THE MEANING OF SUFFERING 141

INTRODUCTION

When is the best time to talk about suffering? When we are not in pain and trouble, we are often not deeply interested in the subject. When we are in suffering, we are often not very rational about it. Perhaps, therefore, it would be better if we adopted the attitude of the London cockney, who, in the dark days of the Dunkerque tragedy, said: "Life ain't all that you want, but it's all that you can 'ave. So stick a geranium in your 'at and be 'appy." Certainly such a spirit sustained many a brave Britisher in the dangerous days of their bombing.

And if we were concerned only about our own pain and suffering, it would be commendable to grin and bear it in silence. But we are members of God's family; and though you and I might be brave enough to keep our troubles to ourselves, we would be cruelly unfeeling if we did not suffer with the hungry, sick, frustrated, oppressed people of the earth. G. A. Studdert-Kennedy, gallant British chaplain in the First World War, said that any person who was undisturbed by the pain and suffering of others was himself suffering either from "hardening of the heart or softening of the brain."

This study has not been prepared merely for those who are puzzled about the mystery of their own misery. It is written for those who are sufficiently Christian to be concerned about the sufferings of others. And young readers, who may not have had much experience of suffering and hence may not be deeply interested, should remember that Romain Rolland said that the comprehension of what is real in art cannot be arrived at except through pain. "Sorrow," he said, "is the touchstone." Certainly sorrow is the touchstone in the art of living. We never appreciate the real values of life until we come to them in trouble.

This little book, therefore, is written for three groups of people: those who are in suffering; those who are concerned about the troubles and sorrows of others; and those, young or old, who are in love with life and want to make the best of it.

In the scale of life, living creatures are graded upward in proportion to their capacity for pain. At the lowest level are such creatures as the worm and the oyster, whose range of feeling is very low. The turtle is somewhat higher, but it is so sluggish and cold-blooded that it probably does not feel much. But the finely-bred dog and the high-spirited horse seem sensitive to the moods of their human companions. And when we rise to the level of man, we find a being who has feelings to be hurt, a conscience to gnaw at him, anxieties to fret him, memories to torture him.

The more highly developed the person, the more sensitive he is to suffering and sorrow. The ear that is most alive to harmony is most hurt by discord. The more one loves, the more he is exposed to the possibility of pain. The conscience that is most responsive to goodness is most shocked by the evils around it, and is the most hard-pressed to explain why the godly suffer.

Our acceptance of suffering, like Christ's, however, will bring not merely conquest over pain but life transcendently resurrected, renewed, transformed. The base metal of experience, tried in the furnace of suffering, becomes transmuted into gold, the coin of the Kingdom.

Christ came to the realization, in the Garden of Gethsemane, that only through the total acceptance of his cross, his own suffering and death, could men be reconciled to God. *His* acceptance of suffering was made, not only for himself, but for all his followers, and for all the sons of man. We, too, must pass through our Gethsemanes and must learn through his example—as we pray for the cup of suffering to pass from us—that somehow we, too, must find the strength to add, "Not my will but thine be done." It is not easy. It is hard. But, in our acceptance, we will see God, and we will find revealed to us the meaning and purpose and values which creative suffering can disclose.

And while this mystery of suffering may not be solved in the earthly sense, it will no longer exist in the sense that it will have become lost in the greater mystery of the awareness of God—"whose ways are past finding out" by finite humanity, but whose infinite love and power are bestowed unstintingly upon his children.

Acknowledgments. In the writing of this book I am indebted, first of all, to Methodist women, who have largely determined its general scope. Even its outline came into being and was structured in response to their requests and questions on the subject of suffering, presented through the Committee on Spiritual Life of the Woman's Division of Christian Service. I am also indebted to Miss Frances Eshelman, editor of the book; to Miss Fanny Alliger for painstaking research; to Mrs. Robert Westall for revealing insights; to Mrs. C. Maud Lynch for careful revision; to Miss Beatrice Meylan, my personal secretary; to Miss Geneva Helm, my sermon secretary; and to the late Miss Marian Marcy, my radio secretary, for faithful service in typing the manuscript; and to my wife, Zellah Endly Sockman, who must have experienced some of "the meaning of suffering" while it was being written.

RALPH W. SOCKMAN

New York, N.Y.
April, 1961

CHAPTER I

The Sources of Suffering

SOURCES OF SUFFERING WE CAN UNDERSTAND

Suffering Due to Sin. It is not possible for people to know how much of their suffering is due to sin. On one occasion Jesus saw beside the road a man blind from his birth. His disciples asked, "Who sinned, this man or his parents, that he was born blind?" Jesus answered, "It was not that this man sinned, or his parents, but that the works of God might be made manifest in him" (John 9:1-3).

At another time some of the listening crowd spoke to Jesus about the Galileans "whose blood Pilate had mingled with their sacrifices." Jesus answered them saying, "Do you think that these Galileans were worse sinners than all the other Galileans, because they suffered thus? I tell you, No; but unless you repent you will all likewise perish." Then he went on to say, "Or those eighteen upon whom the tower in Siloam fell and killed them, do you think that they were worse offenders than all the others who dwelt in Jerusalem? I tell you, No; but unless you repent you will all likewise perish" (Luke 13:1-5).

In the light of Jesus' answers we should not try to trace specific cases of suffering back to their causes in the sins of the sufferers. That effort was the error of Job's so-called friends. The fallacy of ascribing suffering dogmatically to sin was pointed out by a cynical reporter at the time of the San Francisco earthquake when he noted that one of the few buildings spared in the devastated area was a big brewery.

Yet Jesus did make clear that sin is a cause of suffering. On several occasions Jesus prefaced his physical cures with words like these: "Your sins are forgiven you." Perhaps the works of sin were visible in the patient's appearance. Sinful indulgence leaves its evidence in the bleary eyes of the drunkard, the flabby features and frame of the sensualist, the diseased bodies of the unchaste, the ruins of broken homes.

Even those who no longer think of God as a stern judge dispensing penalties can still see that the violation of moral laws carries punishment. When they turn from theology to psychology and biology, the evidence is quite as convincing. Listen to Sigmund Freud: "Nature does not ask us to restrain our instincts, she lets us do as we like; but she has her peculiar effective mode of restricting us; she destroys us, coldly, cruelly, callously, as it seems to us, and possibly just through what has caused our satisfaction." [1] This would seem to be a Freudian endorsement of St. Paul's warning: "Do not be deceived: God is not mocked, for whatever a man sows, that he will also reap" (Gal. 6:7).

Jesus is reported in the Gospels as giving more attention to the sins of the mind than to those of the body. Perhaps the reason is that the former are less visible and more subtle in their devastation. If a person goes out and gets beastly drunk, he makes a spectacle of himself and incurs social rebuke. But the sins of the mind, like pride, envy, and selfishness, may be concealed under the cloak of respectability and invite no censure from others. Hence Jesus had to waken us to the mental sins which outsiders may overlook.

Yet the sins of the mind pull the longest trains of

suffering. They destroy our peace of mind. They may cause mental illness. They poison the springs of virtue. They kill the roots of love. They foster evils which eventuate in immeasurable suffering to others. One unscrupulous greedy, selfish, powerful person can do more harm than a dozen drunken derelicts.

Sin forms bad habits which cause repetitious suffering. Sin leaves a record, sometimes in the courts of law, and always in the chambers of the mind. Sin diffuses an influence which cannot be retracted any more than we can call back the breath which left our nostrils a moment ago. However we may soften the old theological terms, and however sophisticated we may become in our thinking, we cannot escape the old law, "The wages of sin is death" (Rom. 6:23), death to something in us and around us.

Suffering Due to Individual Guilt. Granting that some of our suffering is caused by sin, we ask, "How much is due to our own guilt?"

The ancient Jews had a proverb, "The fathers have eaten sour grapes, and the children's teeth are set on edge" (Ezek. 18:2). It was the figurative way of asserting that the sins of the fathers result in the sufferings of their posterity. But both Jeremiah and Ezekiel warn their countrymen against blaming their ills on the sins of their fathers. Ezekiel says: "This proverb shall no more be used by you in Israel" (Ezek. 18:3). Jeremiah adds: "Every one shall die for his own sin; each man who eats sour grapes, his teeth shall be set on edge" (Jer. 31:30).

That heredity does cause some suffering cannot be denied. And conscience bids us pause on the brink of temptation to ponder the old assertion: "The LORD is slow to anger, and abounding in steadfast love, forgiving iniquity and transgression, but he will by no means clear the guilty, visiting the iniquity of the fathers upon children, upon the third and upon the fourth generation" (Num. 14:18). But while the Scripture warns the fathers against the suffering they may bring on their children, it also cautions the children against offering their fathers' sins as an explanation of their own ills. Each of us must face his own moral responsibility.

Also, we must beware of attributing too much of our pain and trouble to environmental factors. To be sure, we are surrounded by social evils as was the soul of Hamlet by a sea of troubles. It is so easy to dilute our sense of personal guilt by letting in the thought of society's sins. Instead of spending the closing moments of our days in soul-searching prayer, we are so likely to turn on the last news broadcast which shifts our thoughts from our own shortcomings to the bad news of others. We are prone to develop a club-like atmosphere of mutual exoneration. Too many of us are like the first century Corinthians who "measure themselves by one another, and compare themselves with one another" and are therefore "without understanding" (II Cor. 10:12). Whatever the forces which play upon us through heredity and environment, and however well we may compare with our neighbors, there are some points where we must stand and say, "Here I am morally responsible," and some times when we must look up to God in penitence and cry with the psalmist, "Against thee, thee only, have I sinned" (Ps. 51:4).

It is comparatively easy to gallop with the congregation through the Lord's prayer, repeating, "Forgive us our trespasses"; but it is hard soul-searching to cry, "Forgive me my dishonesty, my impurity, my sinful gossip." If we are to get at the source of some of our suffering, we must individualize our guilt, we must cease diluting our own sinfulness with the thought of the moral failings of others, we must sometimes recover the sense of shame which the psychoanalysts have tried to banish. In MacLeish's "J.B." the three "friends" of Job, unlike their Biblical predecessors, try to disprove Job's guilt as a cause of his suffering. But their Marxist and Freudian attitudes do not annul the truth expressed by John: "If we say we have no sin, we deceive ourselves, and the truth is not in us. If we confess our sins, he is faithful and just, and will forgive our sins and cleanse us from all unrighteousness" (I John 1:8-9).

Suffering Due to Collective Guilt. If war were to break out, could we consider ourselves absolutely innocent victims of its suffering? Only if we had done our utmost to prevent it. And how many of us could claim that? War is the whirlwind reaped by those who have sown the wind. And in the sowing of ignorance, ill will, and racial prejudice most of us have been involved at some point. War begins in the minds of men. We cannot put all the blame on dictators and diplomats and munitions-makers.

When we think of our loose words in times of provocation, of our lackluster and listless hours in times of opportunity and challenge, of our aloofness from movements making for peace and righteousness, of our timid silence in times of moral struggle, of our unconcern in the face of suffering and injustice—when we consider all this, who of us is not involved in the collective guilt of our sinful society?

Why was Jesus baptized? Some there are who think that Jesus Christ in becoming man so entered into the limitations of human nature that he felt the need of personal forgiveness and cleansing. It is true that the better a person is, the more he feels his imperfections. But those of us who feel that Jesus was sinless in his own personal life explain his baptism at the hands of John as prompted by his feeling of involvement in the sins of his people. *We believe that he assumed a share in the guilt of his society.*

And certainly, in explaining Christ's crucifixion, we cannot confine the guilt to individuals like Judas and Pilate, or to the Jewish people. The motives and forces which put Jesus to death are as prevalent today as in first-century Palestine, and we are all tainted with the collective guilt. We are all under judgment, and part of our suffering is due to the sinfulness which was climaxed in Pilate's court.

Collective Suffering. While it may be difficult at times to convince us of our collective guilt, there is abundant visible evidence of our collective suffering. No man lives to himself, sins to himself, suffers to himself, or dies to himself. Our sins and sufferings flow together.

On our highways the reckless driver endangers the lives of others and increases the insurance rates of all. We cannot segregate our suffering. Contagious disease is no respecter of persons or of races. We may travel in different social classes as do passengers on a ship, but when the ship strikes an iceberg or bursts into flames, all discover that they are in the same boat.

We may reduce suffering by improved medicine, safety campaigns, and personal precaution, but there still remains an inevitable residuum of pain. Love itself has pain in its heart, sometimes aching with loneliness, sometimes burning with passion, sometimes freezing with despair, sometimes bleeding with loss.

(The more we love, the more we expose ourselves to the possibility of pain)

We are bound together by the words we say, by the thoughts which show in the look of our eyes and the clasp of our hands, by the contagion of our vices and our virtues.

How we are to face this fact will be considered later. Suffice it to say here what the veteran Paul said to young Timothy: "Take your share of suffering as a good soldier of Christ Jesus" (II Tim. 2:3).

Suffering Caused by Our Enemies. The Psalms reveal how much suffering the singers of Israel attributed to their enemies. Typical of unnumbered passages is this: "Deliver me from my enemies. O my God, protect me from those who rise up against me, deliver me from those who work evil" (Ps. 59:1-2). Perhaps the people of Israel were obsessed with the malevolence of enemies because of the oppression inflicted on their nation. But even in a nation which sits near the top of the world the hostility of enemies is a cause of suffering which cannot be ignored.

On the international stage we live in a cold war which causes immeasurable anxiety and threatens to break out in indescribable butchery. How to prevent war is the Number One problem of our time. It is a noteworthy fact, however, that the fear of war seems to cause few nervous breakdowns. It is not our national, but our personal, enemies that seem to get under our skin most painfully. Perhaps this points to our self-centeredness as a contributory cause of our suffering.

As individuals, very few of us are like the old man who said he was at peace with the world because he had outlived his enemies! (Rare is the person who does not have some who are ill-disposed toward him) Yet we suffer more from thinking about the harm our enemies might do to us than from the actual harm they do. And it is very probable that each of us looks upon certain persons as enemies, whereas those individuals are not conscious of any hostility toward us. We interpret as slights many actions which were not so intended. Thus some of our "enemies" may be the creation of imagination and misinformation, and what is needed for our wounded feelings is the aseptic healing of truth. (Also see Chapter 2.)

Suffering Due to Mistakes. Consider the cost of our mistakes. A husband and wife work hard to lay up financial resources for old age. Not knowing investments, they are guided into an unstable enterprise and lose their funds. It is a mistake, and it costs them their retirement security.

I think of a woman who for years has been suffering almost indescribable agony of pain; the ends of her nerves have been affected. She believes that her condition is due to a mistaken diagnosis and treatment given years ago.

The hunting season is on; a party of friends go out to shoot. One of them, seeing a rustling in the brush, mistakes it for the presence of the quarry; he fires and kills a friend. And, though he dedicates his life to make up for it, he never can forgive himself.

Think too, how much costlier mistakes are becoming as the roads become more crowded with cars, the air becomes more filled with planes, and even outer space has its satellites. In 1942, we tested a bomb equal to four tons of T.N.T. In 1945 we dropped a bomb at Hiroshima that was the equivalent of 20,000 tons of T.N.T., and in 1954 we were testing a bomb equal to twenty million tons of T.N.T.

In this nuclear age we are exhausting our margin of error. Think, too, of the increased cost of mistakes in a world which has doubled its population from 1900 to this present time; and the prediction is that at the present rate of increase, there will be at least six billion people on this planet in the year 2000. Add to that fact the possibility that every nation may have nuclear power in its hands. Whether or not we say God punishes us for our mistakes, they are costly and becoming infinitely more so.

How many of our mistakes are due to ignorance! If you drive your car beyond the proper speed and the policeman comes alongside you, it does not quite excuse you to say, "I did not know I was going that fast." To say, "I did not know the gun was loaded," does not clear your conscience if tragedy occurs. No, and ignorance does not excuse you in the eyes of God, according to the Bible. Turn back to Leviticus and read the instructions which Moses gave to his people, and you find these words: "If any one sins, doing any of the things which the LORD has commanded not to be done, though he does not know it, yet he is guilty and shall bear his iniquity" (Lev. 5:17). Turn to the New Testament. Jesus is telling the people the parable of the servant who thought his master was not going to return. He became drunk and beat the other servants, and he was beaten with many stripes. Then Jesus says: "But he who did not know, and did what deserved a beating, shall receive a light beating" (Luke 12:48). Nevertheless, he was beaten! God takes account of the motive, but *he does not excuse for lack of knowledge.*

Familiar is the adage: "The road to hell is paved with good intentions." The havoc wrought by well-meaning but ill-informed and thoughtless people is almost as great as that done by the deliberately bad. (The Christian must look both at the roots of the motive and at the fruits of the results.) Jesus said, "By their fruits you shall know them." We have a moral obligation to look at the situation in which our acts operate just as truly as at the motives of our action. <u>We have a moral duty to be intelligent.</u>

Sources of Suffering We Do Not Understand

Chance. What part does the element of chance play in life? This is a question which will not down. Long centuries ago a realistic writer asserted: "Again I saw that under the sun the race is not to the swift, nor the battle to the strong, nor bread to the wise, nor riches to the intelligent, nor favor to the men of skill: but time and chance happen to them all" (Eccles. 9:11).

No doubt most of us could parallel these observations of Ecclesiastes with some of our own. If we accept the definition of chance as "the unknown or undefined cause of events that to us are uncertain or not subject to calculation," then we have to agree with the Biblical writer that "Time and chance happen to all."

The way we face this factor of chance helps to determine the spirit and quality of our lives. When we count on chance in lieu of preparation and prudence, we weaken our characters. (Jesus rebuked such recklessness by citing the man who began to build without counting the cost and hence was not able to finish) Louis Pasteur discovered the principle of vaccination through the error of an assistant in his laboratory who failed to feed certain cultures properly. When Pasteur was taunted by his critics who said that he had stumbled on his discovery by chance, he replied simply, "True, but chance favors the trained mind."

Also we undo our moral fiber when we count on chance as a short cut to fortune and reward. The demoralizing effect of the gambling spirit may be seen on every side. When it gets into one's blood, it drives out the red corpuscles of vital, vigorous effort.

Still another way in which we allow the element of chance to injure character is to offer it as an alibi for our adversities and perversities. The classic illustration of this is in *King Lear:*

> This is the excellent foppery of the world, that, when we are sick in fortune,—often the surfeit of our own behavior,—we make guilty of our disasters the sun, the moon, and the stars: as if we were villains by necessity, fools by heavenly compulsion; ... drunkards, liars and adulterers, by an enforced obedience of planetary influence; and all that we are evil in, by a divine thrusting on.[2]

By a wrong attitude toward chance we may become reckless fools, ruined gamblers, or futile grumblers.

On the other hand, we may so treat the factor of chance that it calls forth the best in us. For one thing, it helps to beget faith. Following after sure and safe things involves no faith. Also it is the presence of chance that calls forth the non-calculating spirit of true love. (There could be no genuine love in a cut-and-dried world where rewards were guaranteed.)

Furthermore, in this world, our finite minds see "in a mirror dimly," and "know in part"; and what we call chance may be a part of destiny when looked at in the divine perspective. Isaac Foot wrote that if Cromwell or Lincoln had been born ten years earlier or ten years later, the likelihood is that we would never have heard of them. Some might say, therefore, that the presence of Cromwell in the English crisis of 1642 and the appearing of Lincoln in the American crisis of 1861 were mere chance. But both men regarded themselves as instruments prepared and fitted to meet a challenge which they could ignore only at the peril of their souls.

Also, the element of chance may make life at times seem like a lottery on the material level, but not so on the spiritual level. The farmer sowing his wheat may not always get a rewarding crop, but the patience and the resourcefulness which he puts into his work brings forth a harvest of greater patience and resourcefulness. The wise man, as Ecclesiastes said, may not always get wealth in return for his wisdom, but by putting intelligence into his work, he develops more wisdom. In the realm of the spirit, it is true that "whatever a man sows, that he will also reap" (Gal. 6:7).

Accidents. Our lives are affected by accidents. Many can be averted by using care and foresight. But despite precautions and safety campaigns, some accidents do occur to the most careful.

A friend of mine, who had just retired from a long and successful pastorate, was driving with his wife from New York to Asheville, North Carolina. A truck approached at high speed and, just as it reached them, a tire blew out. The truck careened, killing the wife instantly and horribly mangling the husband. How can we explain such a dire calamity befalling two such good people? We are again reminded of the falling of the tower of Siloam which killed eighteen people, and about which Jesus said that the tragedy was not due to any fault of their own. Such is the mystery of evil.

Life is strewn with enigmas like this. But the paths of history are also strewn with sturdy characters who have turned accidents into achievements. Some forty years ago Clarence Charest, who had been playing tennis with moderate success, lost his right arm at about the age of thirty in a hideous hunting accident. His friends commiserated with him, the more because it was his tennis arm and seemingly his playing days were over. But they did not know their man. In the next ten years he taught himself to play tennis with his left hand; and when at 45 he became eligible for the National Veterans Tournament, he won the championship from sixty-three able-bodied competitors, three years out of the next five.

More will be said later about the way to face the unexplained uncertainties of life, but here let it suffice to say that men have come through such things "more than conquerors." They have demonstrated that "suffering produces endurance, and endurance produces character, and character produces hope" (Rom. 5:3).

It is strange but true that the sturdiest hope springs from those who have been dealt the stiffest blows. The glory and gallantry of living is to be able to say with Robert Louis Stevenson:

> To go on forever and fail and go on again,
> And be mauled to the earth and arise,
> And contend for the shade of a word
>   and a thing not seen with the eyes:
> With the half of a broken hope for a
>   pillow at night
> That somehow the right is the right
> And the smooth shall bloom from the rough.[3]

Acts of God. Our legal terminology has made us familiar with another cause of suffering called an "act of God." It is thus defined: "an inevitable event occurring by reason of the operation of nature unmixed with human agency or human negligence." Classed as acts of God are such events as earthquakes, lightning, tempests. These are recognized as legal alibis for the nonperformance of business contracts.

Such unpredictable and inevitable occurrences illustrate the seeming cruelty of nature. C. S. Lewis asserts that in his atheistic days it was the apparently cruel indifference of nature which prevented his belief in God. The earth "is so arranged that all the forms of it [life] can live only by preying upon one another. In the lower forms this process entails only death, but in the higher there appears a new quality called consciousness which enables it to be attended with pain." [4]

Nature does seem "red in tooth and claw." Creation is a curious mixture of stars and snakes, of beauty and poisons, of trade winds that aid commerce and tornadoes that tear up towns and strew the ground with lifeless bodies.

Surely it does seem hard to see the goodness of God who creates typhoons and tetanus germs, blind babies, and idiots. At Lenten services I often hear a prayer containing the words: "O Lord, who hatest nothing that Thou hast made." And I think of rattlesnakes and rats and hyenas. Does God love such creatures? If God is the Creator, he must have a purpose and place for even such as these. I am told that these things serve to maintain the balance of nature. This argument may be of some satisfaction to me philosophically, but it would hardly comfort me if my baby died from a rattlesnake bite.

How much animals suffer in the struggle of nature we do not know. Bodily pain is a lesser element in the range of suffering, and hence the degree of their anguish depends upon the extent to which animals possess sentience and soul. Here again we are in the dark.

How much men suffer from the "acts of God" and the actions of men has been tested by most readers of these pages. But why? The question is as fresh as the morning paper and as old as Eden. The depths of pain were probed by Job, and his experience—when interpreted by Archibald MacLeish[5]—can still pack theaters and win Pulitzer prizes. (His suffering reached such extremity that, in the dust and ashes of his agony, he hears from his wife what MacLeish says are the most dreadful words ever spoken by a wife to a husband: "Curse God, and die" (Job 2:9). But Job still holds on; he will not renounce his faith in God. He still clings to it even during those tedious conversations with his three so-called friends who try to trace his sufferings back to their source in his own sins. But they do not convince Job that he has been guilty.)

Then he hears out of the whirlwind the voice of God saying to him:

"Gird up your loins like a man,
  I will question you, and you shall declare to me."

Then follow some of the most magnificent lines in all literature:

"Where were you when I laid the foundation of
   the earth?"
". . . Who shut in the sea with doors. . .?"
"Where is the way to the dwelling of light,
   and where is the place of darkness. . . ?"
—*Job 38:3, 4, 8, 19*

Of course, Job cannot answer these questions. Therefore, the implication is that if he cannot answer God's questions, why should he expect God to answer his question? Job is not answered. But he is silenced by the very majesty of God. And he ends with these words:

"I know that thou canst do all things,
   and that no purpose of thine can be thwarted.

. . . .

"therefore I despise myself,
   and repent in dust and ashes."
—*Job 42:2, 6*

The climax of the modern play is this: that Job and his wife decide to start all over again. There is in man a force of love that cannot be quenched by the fires of suffering. In that is man's greatness and in that is the secret of his survival. He is going to start over again.

It is a heroic note. We are still at our wit's end, as Job was. But since the time Job lived, Jesus has lived also. And that makes a difference in the picture. With Jesus we do not face suffering in the bleak, stoic attitude. MacLeish says that love "answers life with life and so justifies that bravely tolling line of Shakespeare, that declares 'love bears it out even to the edge of doom.'"

Yes, but St. Paul said something with a little different accent. He said, "Love bears all things, believes all things, hopes all things, endures all things. Love never ends" (I Cor. 13:7, 8). We might say that Job also said this. But listen to what Paul says afterward. "Now we see in a mirror dimly, but then face to face. Now I know in part; then I shall understand fully, even as I have been fully understood. So faith, hope, love abide, these three; but the greatest of these is love" (I Cor. 13:12-13). Paul leaves us at our wit's end, but not at the end of Christian faith, hope, and love. And I am going to suggest one or two directions of thought which I think will take us a little beyond Job.

Suggestions for Further Thought

The first is this: *We can take a more intelligent attitude and have a more intelligent faith in the infinite.* Like Job, our finite minds face the infinite, and we cannot see through, but our sense of the infinite is greater now than Job's was.

Jesus has lived since Job, and it was said of him that he "brought life and immortality to light" (II Tim.

1:10). We not only have enlarged our faith in the infinite by science, but we have, through Christ, lengthened our thinking about life. (We, unlike Job, do not demand to see God's justice demonstrated within the span of the individual's life.) We can think in the larger frame of eternity. Oh, do not misunderstand me! I do not think we should supinely take the injustices of the world and say that God will satisfy them hereafter in heaven. The communist charge, as you know, is that Christians have allowed worldly injustice and suffering to endure because they thought about "pie in the sky, by and by." No, not that!

But here is the thing that Christ does give. He gives a new climate and a new frame for our thinking about justice. St. Paul developed hope through his suffering. He said, "Tribulation worketh patience; and patience, experience; and experience, hope" (K.J.V.). Or, as the Revised Standard Version puts it, "Suffering produces endurance, and endurance produces character, and character produces hope" (Rom. 5:3). It is not true, as the communists say, that people who believe in a future heaven are not going to work to cure the earth's ills. The testimony of history is that it is the people who believe in a larger span of life who have done the most to better the span we have here, because they have been "steadfast, immovable, always abounding in the work of the Lord, knowing that in the Lord . . . labor is not in vain" (I Cor. 15:58).

May I suggest another direction for thought? It is this: *How could we have faith and hope and love without the mystery of suffering?* Suppose that we could calculate every cause of suffering; suppose we could work it out on a factory basis, how much we put in and how much God will reward us for it. We could not have faith on a calculating basis like that. "Faith is the conviction of things not seen" (Heb. 11:1). If you can see them, you do not have faith. Or, take hope. Paul said, "In this hope we were saved. Now hope that is seen is not hope" (Rom. 8:24). When we see hope, that is the end of it. But when we "hope for what we do not see, we wait for it with patience" (Rom. 8:25), and work for it. We cannot have hope without mystery.

And what about love? Think what an adventure into mystery love is. Ponder the marriage service. In the marriage vow we say, "I, John, take thee, Mary, to be my wedded wife, to have and to hold, from this day forward, for better, for worse, for richer, for poorer, in sickness and in health." What uncertainty! Suppose we drew up a marriage contract the way we draw up a sale of property or an insurance policy. Suppose we tried to safeguard ourselves in all the details of home life. Ah, sweet mystery of life! that is what faith is; that is what hope is; that is what love is. Without them life would not be worth living. And without the mystery of possible suffering, there would not be faith and hope and love.

A third line of thought is this: when we ponder it long enough, *the mystery of goodness is even greater than the mystery of suffering*. We are ever talking about the mystery of evil. Why does a good God allow good people to die-young? Why does he allow little innocent babies to be bombed? Why does he allow tornadoes to jump from town to town, leaving strewn bodies in their wake? Well, I cannot explain it, but I will confess that I find it almost easier to explain evil than goodness. Why does a man lay down his life for his friends? Why did a Christ go to the cross to save his enemies? "Gird up your loins like a man" and answer those questions.

C. S. Lewis says that we would not find this problem

of suffering so insoluble if we got a high enough concept of God and of love. We think of God as existing to serve us. That is not his role. We are here to serve God. He is the Party of the first part; we are the party of the second part. Therefore, we should not measure his justice by the way he seems to treat us. That is too small a scale. Furthermore, we should not measure his love by how happy it makes us. What would you think of the love of a friend if he tried to make you happy even when you were dishonest or impure? His love would not mean much, would it? [6] What if God's love meant that, whatever we did, he would coddle us, comfort us, make us feel good? Job leaves the human spirit in the mood which William E. Henley voiced in his poem, "Invictus." Henley, after his long suffering, said:

> Out of the night that covers me,
>   Black as the Pit from pole to pole,
> I thank whatever gods there be
>   For my unconquerable soul.[7]

But Henley wrote later a lovelier poem about

> Night with her train of stars
> And her great gift of sleep.[8]

Somehow he came out of the night that was "black ... from pole to pole" to see a light. It is that gleam of light in the darkness which the Christian faith gives.

Therefore to Job's stoic stand in the darkness can be added the words of one who suffered almost as much as Job—St. Paul—"O the depth of the riches and wisdom and knowledge of God! How unsearchable are his judgments and how inscrutable his ways! ... For from him and through him and to him are all things. To him be glory forever. Amen" (Rom. 11:33-36).

CHAPTER II

The Pain of Living
—How to Face It

In its broad sense we may define pain as the tone of feeling which is the opposite of pleasure. It is the disagreeable in all its degrees and forms. In this chapter we shall consider some mental areas of pain, and leave the physical aspects for the following chapter.

Facing the Unforeseeable

Why is it that when we talk about the unforeseeable uncertainties of life we usually think of the dark aspects of it? We think of accidents which may befall us at any time, of calamities that may come crashing around the corner, of illnesses that may lay us low, of wars that may be sparked by some dictator, or of death that may be lurking we know not where.

But when we read our Bible enough, we see that Jesus taught us that this suddenness of divine intervention may come in glad surprises, just as it may come in floods and lightning flashes. (God would have us realize that there are emergencies of goodness and gladness as well as of calamity and sorrow) Jesus told the story about a bridegroom coming to his marriage feast. In Oriental countries at that time marriages were celebrated at night. It was the custom for the bridesmaids to welcome the bridegroom to the home of his bride. In the story, ten of them came with their lamps;

five were wise enough to bring extra oil; five were foolish and brought no extra supply. The arrival was delayed and they grew drowsy and went to sleep. Then suddenly the approach of the bridegroom was announced and those who had not the extra oil tried to get from the others, but were told to go and buy from the dealers. While they were gone the bridegroom came and "those who were ready went with him to the marriage feast; and the door was shut" (Matt. 25:10). Jesus is trying to tell us that in facing the unforeseeable we must face not only the suddenness of the unexpected, but the delay of the expected; and also, we must face expectantly the surprises of the good as well as the possible surprises of the bad.

Christ would have us look for the best as well as the worst. We have a saying: "Expect the best, prepare for the worst, and take what comes." That may be wise counsel, but it is hard to keep expecting the best when we are preparing for the worst.

We live so much in the atmosphere of distrust and fear that we spend more effort in preparing for the bad than for the good. In fact, the idea of "preparedness" has come to connote getting ready for the worst.

Consider our national life. When we speak of preparedness, we think of the varied and vastly expensive means of military defense which form the overwhelming part of our national budget. We get ready for the worst in other peoples. We talk about the "family" of nations but the irony of such words appears when we think in the analogy of the family. Suppose we trained our children to live together in the family or at school by showing Johnny how to use his Boy Scout knife if a bigger boy threatened or imposed on him, or by giving Mary a packet of pins with which to defend herself if a friend or playmate picked on her.

Oh, I know that is oversimplifying. There *are* gangsters and dictators in the world. There *are* fanatics who are not amenable to reason, and there *are* lawless spirits who have to be restrained. We must prepare against the worst in men. I want to be reasonable. But even reasoning intelligence, as it scans the world, sees the mounting billions being spent preparing against the expected worst in other nations. In comparison, only trifling sums and efforts are being used to learn ways of cooperation between nations, to cultivate understanding between peoples separated by curtains of concealment and prejudice.

There is a law of spiritual gravity in the current methods of international preparedness. When we impute to other people motives lower than our own, we tend to lower our own motives. When we think primarily of preparing against the worst in others, we tend to bring out their worst.

When we prepare for the best, we help to make the best out of the worst. Instead of arguing this point, I should like to call a witness to testify to it. Let us hear the Apostle Paul.

Question: "Paul, what are some of the things which have happened to you?"

Answer: "Five times I have received at the hands of the Jews the forty lashes less one. Three times I have been beaten with rods; once I was stoned. Three times I have been shipwrecked; a night and a day I have been adrift at sea; on frequent journeys, in danger from rivers, danger from robbers, danger from my own people, danger from Gentiles . . . in toil and hardship through many a sleepless night, in hunger and thirst, often without food, in cold and exposure" (II Cor. 11:24-27).

Question: "Yes, Paul, I can see that you have faced

the unforeseeable factors of chance and accidents and the trying tests of adversity. How much did these things hinder you in your life and work?"

Answer: "I want you to know, brethren, that what has happened to me has really served to advance the gospel" (Phil. 1:12).

Question: "Paul, how do you explain your statement that your adversities have aided the advancement of your gospel?"

Answer: "(I have learned, in whatever state I am, to be content.) I know how to be abased, and I know how to abound; in any and all circumstances I have learned the secret of facing plenty and hunger, abundance and want" (Phil. 4:11-12).

Question: "Yes, Paul, we admire and admit the stoic endurance of men like you. But you say you have learned the secret of contentment in such endurance. Can you tell us that secret?"

Answer: "We rejoice in our sufferings, knowing that suffering produces endurance, and endurance produces character, and character produces hope, and hope does not disappoint us, because God's love has been poured into our hearts through the Holy Spirit which has been given to us" (Rom. 5:3-5).

Question: "Paul, as we understand you, the secret of your joyous courage in facing the calamitous events which have befallen you is that through it all you have been sure of God's love. Do not disasters sometimes make you doubt the divine love?"

Answer: "Who shall separate us from the love of Christ? Shall tribulation, or distress, or persecution, or famine, or nakedness, or peril, or sword? ... No, in all these things we are more than conquerers through him who loved us" (Rom. 8:35, 37).

Misunderstanding

One of the most painful features of Jesus' life was that of being misunderstood. Even in his early youth his parents did not fully understand his words and ways. This was shown on the trip to the temple when he was only twelve years old. His presence was missed on the return journey and his parents sought for him anxiously and found him in the temple discussing with the doctors. "His mother said to him, 'Son, why have you treated us so?' . . . And he said to them, 'How is it that you sought me? Did you not know that I must be in my Father's house?'" (Luke 2:48-49) And the record is that they did not understand his saying.

Turn from that early experience to the last words on the cross according to Mark's Gospel: "At the ninth hour Jesus cried with a loud voice, *'Eloi, Eloi, lama sabachthani?'* which means, 'My God, my God, why hast thou forsaken me?' And some of the bystanders hearing it said, 'Behold, he is calling Elijah'" (Mark 15:34-35). In his last agony on the cross, Jesus was misunderstood. And in between, one of the frequently recurring expressions of the Gospels is this, "But they did not understand."

To pour out one's heart to people who do not understand; to bare one's innermost and most precious thoughts to those who have eyes and yet see not; to speak words burning with conviction to those who have ears and yet hear not; to stretch out the arms of love to those in one's own household and find that they do not comprehend; to look down from the cross on the people for whom one is giving one's life; and see not only the hostile stares of those who do not understand—such was the suffering to which Jesus was exposed. And he said that the disciples must also expect to be misunderstood, for "A disciple is not above his teacher, nor a servant above his master" (Matt. 10:24). But at the outset, let us make clear whether we are being misunderstood because we are going Christ's way or because we are not going his way. The willful lad, who thinks his parents do not understand him, because he does not get from them everything he desires, is not misunderstood for Christ's sake. A husband who is wearying of the marital status may fall back on the old cliché, "My wife does not understand me." The truth is that she usually understands him all too well. Just to be misunderstood is no proof of superior virtue. (When a raw recruit is out of step with his squad, his first need is to listen to the music to see if he be at fault.)

We ought also to ask this question: "Do we really want to be understood?" Maybe if those around us really did understand us, they would think less of us than they do now. When we are misunderstood, the first thing is to cleanse our inner motives, so that we are not afraid to have people see us as we really are.

In this matter of misunderstanding we must take into account differences of temperament. There are those who are prosaic in speech and plain matter-of-fact in thought. With such we must speak with literalness and directness. There are others who think with imagination and poetic flights. They may infer meanings we did not intend and we may not rise to their quick insights. A spirit of love makes allowance for these differing types of mind. (Love in the family or in a friendship learns how to sift the chaff of chatter from the wheat of meaning and go on loving despite the weaknesses.)

And however carefully we may watch our words, we can be so easily misunderstood as to our motives. Think how cruelly Jesus' motives were misunderstood. Recall that day when he restored the power of speech to the dumb man. Some of the bystanders said, "He casts out demons by Beelzebul, the prince of demons" (Luke 11:15). How it must have hurt Jesus to have his love thus maligned!

Because it is so difficult to be sure about others' motives, Jesus said: "Judge not, that you be not judged" (Matt. 7:1). Jesus saw the vicious circle of misjudging. Yet, of course, we cannot refrain from making judgments. We cannot sit neutral in the face of flagrant wrong. Jesus was warning against hasty, censorious judgments which do boomerang. Whenever we judge others by appearance, we should do it in the mood of Bobbie Burns' prayer:

> O wad some Pow'r the giftie gie us,
> To see oursels as others see us.[9]

Jesus tried to keep us from pharisaical judgments by his humorous remark about the mote and the beam. We turn to some person and say: "You don't understand me. You are not seeing me right. Let me set you straight." But before we essay to correct his vision, we should cleanse our own eyes of the bias, anger, envy, or whatever keeps us from judging as we should like to be judged.

When our words and motives and deeds are misunderstood, we can usually count on time to clear the vision and correct the estimate. At the Hall of Fame for Great Americans, no person is eligible for election until twenty-five years after his death, thus giving time for the dust of controversy to settle. Truth always has time on its side.

And while time may not always bring true public appraisal, we can be sure of One who understands.

Robert Browning's "Rabbi Ben Ezra" voices the experience:

> Not on the vulgar mass
> Called "work" must sentence pass,
> Things done, that took the eye and had the price;
> O'er which, from level stand,
> The low world laid its hand,
> Found straightway to its mind, could value in a trice;
> But all, the world's coarse thumb
> And finger failed to plumb,
> So passed in making up the main account;
> All instincts immature,
> All purposes unsure,
> That weighed not as his work, yet swelled the man's amount.

Disappointment

One of the most colorful and tragic figures in American history was Benedict Arnold, who displayed such valor in the campaigns around Champlain and Saratoga, and then threw away his laurels by turning traitor. Arnold had the physical courage to face the enemy's batteries, but he had not the fortitude to endure his critics' barbs and the delays to his advancement.

Fortitude is a form of courage almost more rare than physical daring. It has sometimes been called "still courage," or "enduring courage."

If a global war were to break out again and enough of us survived the first nuclear attack, I suppose American manhood would display the same courage it has always shown on the fields of battle. But I sometimes wonder whether we are cultivating fortitude.

Why do I wonder? For one reason, our machine age has given us amazing power to move the movable elements of our environment, but are we learning the self-mastery to endure the obstacles that cannot be removed?

Our medical science, with its anesthetics and its surgery, has banished much of the pain which our ancestors suffered, but are we developing the fortitude to endure the pain that cannot be escaped?

I feel loath to discuss fortitude because I have never demonstrated a sufficient degree of it to give me the right to speak. But I should like to listen with you to the words of one who through peril, toil, and pain earned the right to prescribe. And this veteran of life's vicissitudes, in one of his last messages, the second letter which he wrote to his young recruit, Timothy, says this: "Take your share of suffering as a good soldier of Christ Jesus" (II Tim. 2:3).

We must approach that statement by a first observation, which is this: As a good soldier of Christ Jesus, we are to fight for the removal of suffering. We cannot meekly resign ourselves to many of the pains that our forefathers called the will of God. In such epidemics as the "Black Plague," our ancestors centuries ago said, "This is God's will on a sinning society." And they died by hordes. We should not surrender to disease like that; we should seek to remove its causes. We, as Christians, should augment our efforts to eradicate disease by increasing our support of medical missions, the World Health Organization of the United Nations, and other agencies, seeking to relieve suffering of mind and body.

When people drift into war through narrow nationalism, greed, or indifference, the soldier of Christ should not piously say: "God sent this; this is God's cause." The objective we are seeking may be God's objective, but how far are we ourselves to blame for bringing on the methods we use? (It is not the Christian soldier's place to blame God for the things man has brought on himself) Hence, we are to fight evil and not meekly resign ourselves to it. Weak resignation is not God's will for us.

A good soldier must fight, and when he does fight, it is almost impossible to set a limit to what he can do in the banishment of pain and suffering. In 1865 a relative of mine, then sixteen years of age, was sent home from battle by the doctor's statement that he had but six months to live. He said, "I'll show you," and he did! He lived over sixty years. And he was one of the many in the annals of history who so tackled the seemingly inevitable that they achieved the seemingly incredible.

As good soldiers of Christ, then, we are to fight the evil, the handicaps, the hardships. Yet, even when we do our best, there are still some irremovable obstacles. Paul sweepingly said, "I can do all things in him who strengthens me"—but he could not remove the "thorn in the flesh," his physical ailment. He prayed about it, but it remained. Hence he said, "Take your share of suffering as a good soldier of Christ Jesus" (II Tim. 2:3).

There is something manly about that statement. It suggests first of all that we are to take suffering in the spirit of *soldierliness*. Life has these inexplicable hardships. The tramps may say, "I keep the wind always at my back." But a manly person cannot drift through life like that. To be a man, you must *face* adversity and you should face it with a soldierly bearing.

Some years ago I was with a little group of professional men at lunch in Boston. We were in our late thirties. I raised the question, "How would you characterize the period between thirty and forty?" We had heard so much about youth and its problems. We had read a lot of books on life and other things beginning at forty. But what about the thirties? And one young lawyer gave a reply. It went like this: "It is in the thirties that we learn how to accept ourselves with all our limitations and yet keep our faith in what we are."

(When we thus learn where our limitations are, we use our strength with more intelligence.) We do not keep bruising our hands by beating at the bars of the irremovable. We do not become anxious and worried about things that cannot be changed, for we remember what Jesus said, "Do not be anxious . . . which of you by being anxious can add a cubit to his span of life?" (Luke 12:22-25). These limitations serve us somewhat as the buoys serve the pilot entering the harbor with his ship. He steers between those guiding buoys to keep off the rocks. (So when we learn our limitations, we go on to drive ahead within certain fixed lines and thereby we keep going with soldierly spirit.)

Secondly, we can go on to endure as a good soldier of Christ Jesus with a spirit of good *sportsmanship*. It is one thing to endure suffering grimly; it is another thing to endure it gallantly.

King George V of England was a man not rugged in body, but intrepid in spirit. He once wrote in a message to a boy these words, "In this world, it is not so much doing what we like to do as it is liking what we have to do." It helps greatly to face hardship and disappointment as a part of the game of life.

And when we do stand up to our adversities, we begin to see that the limitations help to make the game of life. The little fellow, learning baseball, is out of sorts when he has to retire from the plate after he has struck out, but as he gets older he learns that the limitation of three strikes helps to make the zest of baseball. The golfer may lose his temper hacking around in the sand traps, but in more mature moments he realizes that the golf course without hazards would be deadly dull. And are we not a bit inconsistent when we spend money to put hazards in our games, and then complain about our Creator putting some hazards in the game of life?

Let us learn what Professor Hocking, formerly of Harvard, had in mind when he said, "Human nature is adapted to mal-adaptation." [10] That is, if life seemed to fit us perfectly, it would not really fit our natures. We develop ourselves because we are in a world which does not seem to fit us.

One of the choicest bits of English literature is the speech that Sir James M. Barrie gave at St. Andrews University in 1922 when he was made Rector of the University. He chose for his subject, "Courage." Barrie, who had written *Peter Pan* and other delightful little dramas, was talking to the students in the aftermath of World War I, against a very grim background. He said that the Almighty "could have provided us with better fun than hard work, but I don't know what it is. To be born poor is probably the next best thing. The greatest glory that has ever come to me was to be swallowed up in London, not knowing a soul, with no means of subsistence, and the fun of working till the stars went out. There was no food in the cupboard, so I did not need to waste time in eating." [11] The humor is there, and the gallant courage. He took his hardship in his stride; he had a spirit of sportsmanship. It is not irreverent to say that the good soldier of Christ Jesus is called to take his share of suffering with the good sportsmanship of one who sees it as part of the game of life.

Kipling's poem, "If," voices the manly attitude:

> If you can force your heart and nerve and sinew
> To serve your turn long after they are gone,
> And so hold on when there is nothing in you
> Except the Will which says to them, "Hold on"!
>
> . . . .
>
> Yours is the Earth and everything that's in it
> And—which is more—you'll be a Man, my son! [12]

But if we are to take our share of suffering as a good soldier of Christ, we need something more than self-discipline. One must be sustained by a Power higher than himself, by One who stands by when there is no one around.

Anxiety

If someone walked up to you and said, "You haven't a thing in the world to be anxious about," what would you reply? I can imagine some answers such as these:

"My dear fellow, you do not know my situation. I have just come from my doctor and he has ordered me to the hospital next week for some X-rays. I fear what he is going to find."

Or, "My father is in Florida and has just been stricken with virus pneumonia. Of course, I am anxious about him."

Or, I hear a woman answer: "I am in an intolerable business situation. I do not see how I can stay much longer, but at my age where can I get another job?" What is a woman to do when she nears the deadline of employability? Is that not something to be anxious about?

Or, who of us does not feel like saying: "Every thoughtful person is bound to have some anxiety about the world situation. The man who is not distressingly concerned about the threat of communism, about the tension between races, about the widening rift between the Orient and Occident—well, such a person is inexcusably shallow or even subnormal!"

Rabbi Liebman was right in his book *Peace of Mind* when he said that "man has to pay the price of fear and worry in order to be human." The patterns of our fears may vary, but "basically all men and women in one degree or another feel guilty, dread pain, suffer loneliness," are anxious about some wrong things they have done in the past, and "seek reassurance" for the future.[13] And in our time, personal fears and worries have been so intensified by public disorders that ours has been called The Age of Anxiety.

Perhaps before going further we ought to distinguish anxiety from some of its kin in the family of fears. Anxiety is uneasiness or distress of mind regarding some uncertain event which may involve danger or misfortune. Anxiety is akin to *anguish* which comes from the same verbal root. Anxiety, however, is mental; anguish may be mental or physical. Anxiety is in regard to the unknown; anguish is in regard to the known.

Anxiety has a weaker sister, known as worry, which is more petty and restless. Anxiety may be quiet and silent; worry is likely to communicate with all around.

Anxiety has a still weaker sister, called fretting, which is a futile complaining without thought of accomplishing or changing anything, but merely as a relief to one's own disquiet.

Thus we see that anxiety is more dignified and deep-seated than worry or fretfulness. Hence it is more serious in its consequences and more difficult to cure. We may snap a person out of a fainting fit by a dash of cold water, but to cure anemia we must build up the blood stream. Similarly we may help to stop people from worrying and fretting by little homely correctives and obvious advice; but to find strength in time of real anxiety we must go more deeply. The worrier can take himself in hand and help to check his fretting by self-control, but when we are in deep anxiety we need to put ourselves in God's hand. And that is what the First Epistle of Peter tells us in the fifth chapter: "Cast all your anxieties on him [God] for he cares about you" (I Peter 5:7).

How does God help in time of anxiety? First he *throws light on the cause of our anxiety*. Psychologists and psychiatrists proceed on the principle that the source of a fear must be found as the first step to its cure. If the roots of an obsession or anxiety can be dug up and brought to light, they will often dry up.

Thus it has been found that, for instance, the fear of closed places can be traced to some childhood experience such as being locked in a dark room or being caught in a culvert. Or, an inferiority complex may be the result of a child's feeling that his parents are so vastly superior. Or, perhaps it derives from the too high standards, perfectionism, which parents set for him and which he can never attain. Sometimes trained practitioners are needed to uncover these long-buried sources of our mental disorders. I have great respect for many sincere and able psychologists and psychiatrists. Of course, in these fields as in all others, even in the ministry of religion, there are charlatans.

Christ, the supreme mental physician, looks first of all to see whether we are anxious about something inside ourselves or outside ourselves. If the basis for the worth of a man's life does not lie within him, then he is at the mercy of events outside himself and often of forces beyond his control. The net result is deep-seated anxiety. If the basic concern of your life is for inner values, like character, integrity, purity, then you do not need to be anxious about what others say about you or do to you. They can smear your reputation, but they cannot change your character. Others can charge you with dishonesty, but they cannot convict your soul. Hence, if we spend our energy in achieving inner qualities rather than in acquiring external things, we put our security beyond the reach of many a fear.

Such was the security Jesus craved for his followers when he bade them "lay up for yourselves treasures in heaven, where neither moth nor rust consumes and where thieves do not break in and steal" (Matt. 6:20). He was speaking of the kingdom of heaven which is here and now and not merely a future state, although we should remember that the qualities of character which we achieve here are the only properties we can take with us into the hereafter. Are we anxious about what may happen to us? Let us start with Christ and look at what is happening *in* us. Let us keep the treasury of our real worth inside ourselves, where it will not be at the mercy of moth, rust, thieves, or circumstances.

"A man's life does not consist in the abundance of his possessions," said our Lord (Luke 12:15). According to Jesus, the richness and fullness of a man's life depend on the worth of the interests which possess him. If we live by the law of grab, we are bound to be anxious and end up empty. If we live by the law of growth, fulfilling the nature God gave us, we shall be free from many fears and full of much contentment.

A second way God helps us in time of anxiety is that he gives *length to our vision*. Jesus said, "Do not be anxious about tomorrow" (Matt. 6:34). My understanding is that he did not mean us to close our eyes to the morrow, but to look beyond it to the longer future. When a person is learning to drive a motor car, his tendency is to focus his eyes at such short range that he sees the road too immediately near. His pace is jerky, his stops are abrupt, his grip is tense. But the experienced driver levels out his gaze, gauges his distance, relaxes his grip, steers steadily and smoothly. So Jesus would have his followers relax some of their tensions and anxieties by longer perspective.

Moreover, the lengthened vision God gives us makes us remember that moods are temporary. The sea of life is swept by waves of emotion which have both their trough and their crest. Even the most even-tempered of us have days when we are down. But when the godly man is down in the trough of depression or moodiness, he steadies himself with the thought that the crest of the wave is coming. Such was the confidence of St. Paul when he said: "For I consider that the sufferings of this present time are not worth comparing with the glory that is to be revealed to us" (Rom. 8:18).

Furthermore, when we catch God's longer vision, we do not try to bear tomorrow's burdens today. There is an Oriental proverb which runs: "He is miserable who feels it, but twice who fears it before it comes." No man's constitution is strong enough to carry today's duties and tomorrow's anxieties piled on top of them. We do not try to eat and drink for tomorrow, yet we so often try to bear the troubles of tomorrow as well as those already with us.

It was to check this tendency of borrowing future cares that Jesus said: "Do not be anxious about tomorrow. . . . Let the day's own trouble be sufficient for the day" (Matt. 6:34). And he might have added the Old Testament promise, "As your days, so shall your strength be" (Deut. 33:25).

Yes, and when we get God's longer perspective, we gain confident strength not only for the days but also for the years. If our faith depends on each day's headlines, we are bound to be anxious about tomorrow's world. Now is the time to catch the Psalmist's longer view and say: "I will lift up mine eyes unto the hills, from whence cometh my help. My help cometh from the LORD, which made heaven and earth" (Psalm 121:1-2, K.J.V.).

Persecution

Only those who have been subjected to persecution are qualified to write about it. Inasmuch as I have never suffered much persecution, I should perhaps remain silent. But I do offer a few observations.

Few ills of life are harder to bear than that of being picked on. I recall a neighbor lad in my boyhood community. He was not very quick-witted. He was a bit awkward in his physical movements. He had a penchant for doing things in the wrong way. Thus he was a ready target for the devilish tendency of boys to find someone to pick on. To make matters worse, his father was an irate individual who was ever rushing in to defend him. The poor lad became the butt of numerous pranks which made his life miserable. His misery could have been relieved greatly by a sense of humor on his parent's part and a more manly indifference to petty slights on his part.

Ernest Ligon quotes an old saying: "The measure of a man is the size of the thing it takes to get his goat." [14] Littleness of spirit invites petty persecutions.

We must always beware of a persecution complex. When we feel that we are being unjustly criticized or attacked, we should first look at ourselves to see if we are unintentionally giving cause for criticism. Some years ago a minister resigned his pulpit under parish pressure. Many of his ministerial colleagues sympathized with him for we thought he was under fire for his courageous social attitudes. One of his laymen, however, issued a thought-provoking statement on the situation. He wrote to this effect: "We did not object to what Dr——— said, but to what he left unsaid. He kept harping on one or two social themes, and never preached about prayer, or hope, or personal salvation." It would seem that the minister had been criticized for some utterances and then he continued to pick at the wound, neglecting the other aspects of his gospel message. A persecution complex distorts one's perspective, inflames the hurt already inflicted, and prevents an approach to reconciliation.

Also, a Christian should realize the futility as well as the wrongness of trying to counter persecution by retaliation. Bishop Gerald Ensley tells a story reported of Sir Winston Churchill. In a gathering where Churchill was present, a speaker was developing at length the idea that the only way to survive in this world is to retaliate, eye for eye, tooth for tooth, bomb for bomb. After the address, Sir Winston sidled up to the speaker and said, "Did you ever try to sting a bee?" [15]

It takes more than self-reliance and self-restraint to sustain one's spirit unbroken and unembittered under persecution. The story of Joseph's mistreatment by his brothers makes the reader's blood boil. Suffering his brothers' jealousy and sold into slavery, Joseph had every reason for the bitterest resentment. The secret of his magnanimity is revealed in his final word to his brothers when at last they were in his power: "As for you—you meant evil against me; but God meant it for good to bring it about that many people should be kept alive, as they are today. So do not fear. I will provide for you and your little ones" (Gen. 50:20-21). Faith in God's overruling providence relieves the pain of present persecution.

It was faith in God's continuing grace which enabled Frederick W. Robertson to endure the whips and scorns which assailed him as a Christian minister in the days of England's industrial revolution. He was persecuted for being too liberal and too aggressive. A brilliant preacher, he died in the middle of the strife for labor reform, at the age of thirty-five. James R. Blackwood, writing of a sermon Robertson preached on "The Loneliness of Christ," in which "he stressed the grandeur of Christ in loneliness and the strength of every solitary life," says: "He was preaching to himself as well as to others who had endured hardness for Christ, not in the heat of the battle but in chilly isolation when called on to fulfill a duty that others looked on coldly, or to stand by a truth that had not yet found welcome in other hearts." Yet he faced his aloneness without fear, "knowing that the Father was with him." [16] Robertson is now regarded as one of the most formative preachers of the nineteenth century, and revered by his colleagues.

Probably no form of persecution is as hard to bear as that due to race, because no person can change his color. When others assail us for our words or deeds, we can examine ourselves and perhaps correct our views or positions. But when we are harassed for our race, we are helpless. The pain may be eased somewhat by the consciousness that increasing numbers of enlightened persons are rising above race prejudice. When Countee Cullen was invited to read his poems before a woman's club, but denied the courtesy of taking tea with the members, a witty observer wrote: "Poems are made by fools like me, but only God can come to tea." Such satire is bound to be a powerful ally of justice in breaking down racial barriers in time, but hope for the future does not take away all the sting of the present.

We need the grace of God to keep our hearts free from resentment against those who wrong us. Once a white reporter, seeking an interview with Roland Hayes, the great Negro tenor, found him eating his meal in a dingy room because the hotel management had denied him access to the dining-room. The reporter exploded in anger, but the singer remained unperturbed. He explained that his earliest singing teacher, also a Negro, had warned him of the slights he would have to encounter as a black artist, and had counselled him not to allow "the barbs of antagonism and insult" to penetrate his soul. This teacher told him that, if his heart was right and his spirit divinely disciplined, nobody in all the world would be able to hurt him. Roland Hayes discovered this to be true. As he tried "every moment of every day to live in such awareness of the divine" that no bitterness could enter his heart, (he learned that nobody in all the world could hurt him except himself.)

When a person can attain such an attitude, he has escaped from the imprisoning bitterness of mind and heart. In the words of Henry van Dyke:

> Self is the only prison that can ever bind the soul.
> Love is the only angel who could bid the gates unroll,
> And when he comes to call thee, arise and follow fast;
> His way may lie through darkness, but it leads to light at last.[17]

However intense the pain of our persecution, we can always be mindful of One who suffered still more, and yet was able to say from his cross, "Father, forgive them for they know not what they do" (Luke 23:34). Rooted and grounded in love, we "may have the power to comprehend with all the saints what is the breadth and length and height and depth, and to know the love of Christ which surpasses knowledge" (Eph. 3:18-19).

CHAPTER III

Physical and Mental Illness

PAIN

Physical pain is by no means the bitterest drop in the cup of suffering. Some forms of bodily discomfort are almost pleasurable. C. S. Lewis testifies: "No one minds the process 'warm—beautifully hot—too hot—it stings' which warns him to withdraw his hand from exposure to the fire: and if I may trust my own feeling, a slight aching in the legs as we climb into bed after a good day's walking is, in fact, pleasurable." [18]

Professor Carl Michalson has pointed out that "the human tolerance to physical punishment is staggering." "Given the proper psychological motivation," he writes, "mere pain precipitates no crisis. A football coach once gave me the prime qualification for a first-class player: 'he must enjoy pain.' The sport never wants for candidates who seem qualified." [19]

And pain leaves no poisonous or perpetuating germs. "When it is over, it is over, and the natural sequel is joy. . . . After an error you need not only to remove the causes . . . , but also to correct the error itself; after a sin you must not only, if possible, remove the temptation, you must also go back and repent the sin itself. In each case an 'undoing' is required. Pain requires no such undoing. You may need to heal the disease which caused it, but the pain, once over, is sterile." [20]

When William Gladstone died after a long and painful illness, Baron von Hügel, the saintly Roman Catholic writer, wrote to Gladstone's daughter expressing not only great admiration for the statesman's brilliant achievements but also recognition of his character and faith during his suffering. He concluded with these words: "I have always loved to think of devoted suffering as the highest, purest, perhaps the only quite pure form of action: and so it was a special grace that one as devoted and as active as your Father, should have been allowed and strengthened to practise the most devoted action possible for a sentient and rational creature of God." Commenting on this letter, William Adams Brown writes, "No one but a Christian could have written that letter." [21]

We do not need to believe that all suffering is sent by God to test us; but whatever its cause, it does test the fineness of our nature. And in facing our pain, we have the superbly helpful example of the finest and most sensitive personality in history.

Jesus bore his suffering with healthy-mindedness. He was indeed "a man of sorrows and acquainted with grief." But he was never gloomy. He never allowed his sufferings to diffuse depression. He had no kinship with those who keep their ailments ever before them. Sometimes when you greet a fellow with the familiar "How are you?" he mistakes the greeting for a question and begins to tell you all his aches and pains. He gives you an organ recital of his ailments, beginning with his heart, his stomach, and then goes on to all the other organs flesh is heir to!

Well, the Master never allowed his sufferings to lead to self-pity nor to invite pity from others. He was so healthy-minded that men, even little children, were glad to be with him.

Also Jesus bore his suffering with dignity. Of all the noble spectacles the race has given us, none can compare with the dignity of our Lord's bearing during his last painful days.

Moreover, Jesus was master of pain. As a physician he sought to banish from men all needless pain. But when it came, he stood up to it. He never allowed pain to make his words petulant, nor frustration to fray his temper. Jesus prayed that the cup of suffering might pass from him, but when he saw that it was necessary, he drank it—drank it with the smile of a winning sportsman, saying to his comrades—"Be of good cheer, I have overcome the world" (John 16:33). Jesus endured the indescribable pain of the cross without becoming bitter toward those who inflicted it, saying, "Father, forgive them; for they know not what they do" (Luke 23:34). Never did man rise above suffering with dignity like unto that of our Lord.

A fine surgeon of my parish succumbed some years ago to cancer. During the excruciating pain of his illness he told me that he had discovered one secret which helped him. Since the mind can hold only one thing at any precise moment, he held his mind to thoughts which crowded out the pain.

Betsey Barton, herself the victim of an accident which paralyzed her legs, had the added agony of watching her mother fight a losing battle with cancer. Her mother, summoning all her courage, kept saying, "I must try a little harder." She would smile and spark her will power. Finally Betsey could not stand it any longer and burst out with the confession: "I have hated your having to learn what I had to learn, Momsie. . . . That is, that will power can only do so much, that's the hardest thing to learn of all." [22]

But when a sufferer has reached the hard realization of will's impotence, there is still a Higher Help. Anne Douglas Sedgwick, the novelist, wrote in a letter during a painful illness: "Now, added to everything else, I can't breathe unless lying down, my ribs collapse. Yet I can't drink my food unless sitting up. Life is a queer struggle. Yet it is mine and beautiful to me. There is joy in knowing I lie in the hands of God. When you wrote, 'Your spirit can surmount anything,' I felt a strange tremor of response, from an indomitable thread of life within me. It is mine, but I feel it communicated from God." [23]

Anne Sedgwick had discovered that the human will and the divine will cannot be definitely separated, for, as Paul said, they work as allies: "Work out your own salvation with fear and trembling; for God is at work in you, both to will and to work for his good pleasure" (Phil. 2:12-13).

This awakened awareness of divine help in pain was expressed by my friend J. Hartley Fowler, the well-known Y.M.C.A. leader. After a severe coronary attack, he wrote a letter to his friends in which were these words:

> I have had a rendezvous with death,
>   and found there is nothing to fear.
> I have had a rendezvous with God,
>   And found Him near.
> I have had a rendezvous with friends,
>   and found them dear.[24]

When we confront inescapable pain, trustful acceptance is better than pale, pious resignation. Still better is it to cooperate with God in transforming one's own suffering into service for others. A few years ago I visited an honored ministerial colleague, the Reverend Henry Relyea. He was in the hospital stricken with cancer. He was not rebellious. Nor did he talk about being resigned. He seemed to feel that as a good soldier of Jesus Christ he had to bear his share of the world's inexplicable suffering. And he was doing it bravely without bitterness. But he was doing more. He was letting the surgeons use his body as a testing ground for some painful experiments, which it was hoped would further the cure of cancer. He was cooperating with God. In his presence I felt humbled and yet immeasurably helped. The expression in his eyes as I left him has lingered through the years. He was "more than conqueror" through Him who loved him.

Disability

A few years ago a very attractive young woman was severely stricken with polio. As she lay in an iron lung her life was despaired of. Her luminous black eyes, as she looked out from her iron bed, made one think of a sorely stricken deer. To the words of the visiting minister she made no answer. Later she smilingly confessed that she interpreted the visit of a minister who had come to give her communion as the offering of the last rites of the church and she was not ready for that. Her youthful, vigorous spirit had not surrendered in the struggle for recovery.

She was the daughter of a doctor and she was not unduly frightened by the initial approaches of the polio. A cousin had been infected with the germ at the age of seven and had come through without much impairment. She was sustained in hope by the thought of others who had improved. She bore her discomfort with such fortitude that she did not want to interrupt the vacation plans of her parents or the work of her devoted young husband.

But, as in the case of so many sufferers, the continued disability proved far harder to bear than the initial pain. Some six years later she reached a plateau of spiritual disillusionment. She did not seem to be making progress in the handling of her body. As she put it, she felt trapped. She lost hope. She became a bit rebellious. She put herself into the hands of a Christian psychiatrist. Through the aid of her family, her church friends, and psychiatric guidance she got back on the track again. Now she is resuming her place of leadership in parish activities. She is walking with ever improving gracefulness. She is effectively and winsomely helping others in overcoming their handicaps. She gives great credit to the cooperation of the church and its members, for through them she has been guided into the deeper meanings of life.

One can endure almost any pain of the moment if he believes it is temporary. But it takes more fortitude and grace to keep up one's spirit in the face of a disability which threatens to be permanent. Every person of mature years can understand the experience of the Englishman, James Payn, who, when overtaken by deafness and illness, wrote his moving essay entitled, *The Backwater of Life*. He said, "It is a strange feeling to one who has been immersed in affairs, and as it were, in the midstream of what we call Life, to find oneself in its Backwater; crippled and helpless." [25]

It is hardly necessary to explain that man's situation. The momentum of his active years still keeps urging him on. But, handicapped by his pain and infirmity, he cannot swing out into the current of affairs again. (His illness makes him feel helpless, and his helplessness intensifies his illness.) Thus the cause creates a result which in turn reacts to heighten the cause. Round and round go his thoughts in one of life's vicious circles.

There are various comforting thoughts which can be planted in the minds of disabled persons, provided they are born of genuine sincerity and deep sympathy. One should think twice and feel deeply when he repeats to a handicapped person what the young prince said to the spastic boy: "You must be God's favorite pupil. He gave you the hardest problem."

Carl Michalson, who cites this incident, vehemently rejects the idea "that suffering and pain are *sent by God* as character-builders or as avenues of artistic insight." Yet out of pain and suffering patiently borne have come fruits of the spirit and creative energy. We should not glibly say that God sends disabilities and accidents to develop us. But we can honestly assert that God's demands upon us, which may be hard and painful, can prove his best gifts to us.[26]

When delays halt our man-made plans and illness or calamity stops us in our programs, may we have the grace and insight of John Ruskin who likened these pauses to the "rests" in a musical score. Ruskin wrote: "Not without design does God write the music of our lives. Be it ours to learn the time, and not be discouraged at the rests. If we say sadly to ourselves, 'There is no music in a rest,' let us not forget there is the making of music in it. The making of music is often a slow and painful process in this life. How patiently God works to teach us! How long He waits for us to learn the lesson!"[27]

Nevertheless, I think Ruskin was more practically helpful when he gave some concrete suggestions about making "nests of pleasant thoughts" from which we fly into whatever the dark days may bring. He listed such things as bright fancies, satisfied memories, noble histories, faithful sayings, treasure houses of precious and restful thoughts, which care cannot disturb, nor pain make gloomy, nor poverty take away from us.

47

These are houses built without hands for our souls to live in. And best of all is the Book of Books.

In these nests of thoughts from which our minds can fly forth into dark experiences can be placed the heartening examples of the gallant souls who have turned their disabilities into creative abilities.

Consider the case of Henry Fawcett who was Postmaster General of England seventy-five years ago. He was graduated with high honors from Cambridge University in 1856. Two years later he was completely blinded by an accident. Friends gathered around and tried to comfort him. All their kindness could not arouse him from his depression. But his university tutor wrote him a letter in a different vein. Instead of merely trying to comfort him, the tutor exhorted him to effort and reminded him that his calamity showed that he was being treated as equal to life's emergencies. The letter included a plan for hard and systematic study. The tutor's help was a gift, although it came in the form of a demand, for it aroused the sleeping power within the blinded man, and started him toward high public service.

Examples of those who have made their handicaps into bundles of power could be multiplied indefinitely. The contagion of their achieving spirit is caught when we expose our minds to the reasoning of Milton in his blindness:

> "Doth God exact day-labor, light denied?"
> I fondly ask. But Patience, to prevent
> That murmur, soon replies, "God doth not need
> Either man's work or his own gifts. Who best
> Bear his mild yoke, they serve him best; his state
> Is kingly: thousands at his bidding speed,
> And post o'er land and ocean without rest:
> They also serve who only stand and wait."
> *John Milton*, ON HIS BLINDNESS

Mental Illness

Jesus was confronted frequently by persons described as possessed of evil spirits. How those cases of mental disorder would be diagnosed by modern medical science, we cannot be sure. But, in the first century as in the twentieth, minds possessed by an idea or an anxiety had a devilish tendency to get going around in circles. Mental derangement is not a derailment of thought which throws it off the track and stops it. It is rather a failure of the mental switches to work, with the result that the trains of thought go round and round instead of ahead toward the main business and some intelligent conclusion. The trouble with sick minds is not that they stop thinking, but that they think in circles. And these vicious circles of mental action may vary in degree from inwardly concealed worry to openly labeled insanity.

How does the Great Physician help us to break these vicious circles of thought? Well, for one thing he would have us exert our wills. We sometimes say to a person who has gotten into a groove of depression or bad thinking, "Snap out of it." It is not the whole cure, but it does something. Jesus recognized that a person through his own will power can control, in part, at least, the doors of his mind. Jesus counselled his followers repeatedly about closing the gates of thought behind them so that yesterday's yelping pack of hounding worries and regrets might not come in to spoil today's peace of mind.

Toward this end he told his followers to "remember Lot's wife." Her weakness, as you may remember from the Old Testament account, was that she kept looking back when she should have been looking forward. Or recall the would-be disciple who first asked that he might go back and bury his father. To this Jesus gave the reply: "Leave the dead to bury their own dead" (Matt. 8:22). It was our Lord's enigmatic way of saying, 'Cut your thought loose from the things you can't do anything about.'

Yet potent as the will is in opening and closing the doors of the mind, Jesus relied even more on the power of the imagination to deliver men from imprisoning and torturing thoughts.

Recall that sullen and disheartened woman who came to draw water at the well where Jesus was resting. She was full of bitterness as she hashed over in her mind the harsh looks and words which she had received because of her none-too-good way of living. Jesus soothed and cooled her festering resentments by setting her thinking about God and his goodness and eternal life. The Great Physician worked on the principle of a certain wise doctor who prescribed for a patient that she should go away and see something big. This woman was allowing her household cares with all the petty details to wear her down. She needed to break the vicious circle of her thinking by getting out of herself, and the doctor felt that this could be done by the sight of some great work of nature, like Niagara or the Grand Canyon.

Robert Louis Stevenson, from the battlefield of his bed, broke the vicious circles of gloomy thought, and sent his mind forth to rove the realms of beauty and adventure. What schoolboy reading the thrilling scenes of *Treasure Island* would have guessed that they were written by a man on a sick bed? Yes, there is a power within us able to change our minds even when we cannot change our places. And our Lord would lead us out of our petty circles of personal anxiety or prejudice or ambition to behold something big.

There are so many causes and phases of mental illness that any adequate treatment here is beyond the bounds of our space. And there is so much attention given to psychiatry and peace of mind that we need hardly discuss symptoms and preventive measures. Dr. Robert D. Hershey quotes a quatrain in which the writer says that since he has joined a "Don't Worry Club," he is "worried most to death" for fear he will worry.[28]

Perhaps a few "common sense" suggestions might be in order.

A few years ago in Los Angeles, I heard a brilliant woman address a luncheon group of ministers' wives. She was pointing out the fact that, while modern mechanical improvements have made the work of women physically easier, there has been an increase of nervous and mental ills. She reminded her hearers that scrubwomen seldom, if ever, have nervous breakdowns. And she might have added for her male listeners what I have often heard doctors say, that ditch-diggers seldom, if ever, have heart trouble.

The speaker's diagnosis was that we nervously exhaust ourselves by a too continuous use of our small muscles. Her prescription was that we should use our larger muscles more. We should change occasionally from the little mincing steps of the living room to the long strides of a brisk walk or even to a stiff climb. We should get down on our knees once in a while or climb up and paint the kitchen ceiling. Homely advice, do you say? Perhaps, but it is a sound principle that we aid in the resting and restoring of our bodily well-being by using our larger muscles.

This principle applies to the mind and spirit as well as to the body. And the proposal to use our larger functions of mind and body is a healthy corrective to some current tendencies. Very popular in many quarters is the interpretation of religion as a mere relaxing from tension. In trying to use religion to make us feel good, we must remember that while the Great Physician did say, "Come to me, all who labor and are heavy-laden, and I will give you rest," he added, "Take my yoke upon you, and learn from me" (Matt. 11:28-29). Christ does comfort as no other can. He does bring rest to weary minds and bodies. But the comfort which he gives comes basically from being yoked with him to interests and tasks so big that they bring into use our largest muscles and powers—aye, they bring into use a strength we do not know we have.

Consider one or two situations in which our minds lose their grip and their step.

Recently, I saw a man who is growing a bit senile. It was sad to contrast his present condition with the personality I knew in the prime of his strength. His memory is slipping. He, who once dealt in large interests, now occupies his mind with little chores. He lives in a world which seems to be growing smaller and he uses less and less of his mental powers.

But now let God take hold of a life like that. Then the failing eyes are opened to vistas beyond those little chores and fences. Like St. Paul, he cultivates the habit of looking at the things that are invisible and eternal rather than the things that are seen and temporal. Though his "outer nature" is decaying, God can make him feel that his "inner nature" is growing day by day (II Cor. 4:16). And thus, instead of pottering around with waning strength, he becomes a potter, shaping a life where "moth and rust do not consume." Yes, there is a vast difference between just pottering around and being a purposeful potter. And that is the difference God makes when age loosens our physical and mental grip.

But this failure of mental grip is by no means limited

to old age. Many younger persons lose their mental grip by distraction. Their minds become so flustered that they cannot fasten onto the main issues of a situation. Their thoughts run off in all directions. They go around in circles. And then God takes hold and does for them what Jesus did for Martha that day when he came to visit and found her so distracted. Jesus said, "Martha, Martha, you are anxious and troubled about many things; one thing is needful. Mary has chosen the good portion, which shall not be taken away from her" (Luke 10:41-42). However confusing the situation, however many things are waiting to be done, there is always some one thing that should come first. And God helps us to regain our mental grip by putting first things first, and then lesser things fall into place. As Jesus said, "But seek first his kingdom and his righteousness, and all these things shall be yours as well" (Matt. 6:33).

Or our minds may lose their grip by running in grooves as well as by being distracted in too many directions. Our thoughts may run along in a narrow channel of self-interest, concerned only about the things close to us. And when our train of thought is in a tunnel of self-centeredness, it seems to be going much faster than it really is. In this we resemble a railroad train which in the tunnel seems to be dashing at terrific speed, but when it comes out into the open and you look from the window at distant landmarks, you see it is not going so fast after all.

Or consider how our minds lose their grip when numbed by sorrow. One of the most comforting passages at funeral services is that from the 121st Psalm: "I will lift up mine eyes unto the hills, from whence cometh my help. My help cometh from the LORD, which made heaven and earth" (Psalm 121:1-2, K.J.V.). The hills lift our thoughts, lengthen our gauge, strengthen our spirits. And we look up from the valley of the shadow of death to the sunlit peaks of eternal hope.

But, of course, any worthwhile discussion of mental illness must deal with its deeper and more tragic phases. One of the tragedies of history is that mental disorders should have gone so long untended. Only a little more than a century ago a school teacher in Boston, retired because of tuberculosis, began a crusade for the treatment of the mentally ill. In 1841 Dorothea Lynde Dix volunteered to teach Sunday school in the East Cambridge jail. There she met for the first time the mentally ill, who in those days were kept in jails and almshouses. She was moved with compassion and set out to change the situation.

Dorothea Dix examined the entire problem with a fresh, keen intelligence that soon made her an authority in the field. She was instrumental in founding or transforming twenty mental hospitals in fifteen states and extended her work into Canada. At each quinquennial election to the Hall of Fame for Great Americans, her name receives an increasing number of votes. She will probably be installed in the Hall of Fame before many years. The mounting recognition of her service is a measure of the rising interest in the treatment of the mentally ill.

So difficult is it for a normal person to peer into the inner recesses of an ill mind that perhaps the better insights will be given by hearing the testimony of one who has been in the depths of despond and has now climbed far enough out to analyze his experiences and point some paths of escape. The one from whom the following quotations come is a Yale graduate with a record of war service as a naval officer.

"Through having strong desires blocked, one can

get into a state of despondency such that one wishes one were dead; then, if efforts to kill oneself are blocked, one feels that someone is taking a great delight in blocking both the initial desires and death, and in fact keeping a person alive solely for the cruel satisfaction of seeing his desires thwarted and observing the agony of mind which ensues.

"Now these periods of true despondency and utter misery were accompanied by sensations of great fatigue and total inability to do hardly anything but attempt to rest; deep inner brain tensions were felt, and, at times, feelings as though an actual war was raging in one's own mind and nervous system.

"My thinking now sees all this as a form of hell of which the main characteristic is the absence of any experience of the meaning of love.

"When one becomes aware that the tormentor [depression] described above is a hidden part of one's own nature, that one has in some way tormented others in the past; then a new level of inner peace comes, a new level of humility, and with it comes a new desire to so love God and his creation that one can truly feel oneself a servant of God.

"Apparently the state I have described is the bottom —or part of the bottom—of the universe. I cannot help but feel that experiencing one form of the total absence of love is in some way the lever or base for the true experience of love and for eventually becoming a being who actually can love in the most perfect sense of the word possible for man.

"This, I feel, is what suffering has meant to me. I suspect that there is more suffering of one sort or another to come until I have truly grown and developed in the spirit of love. The great need is for us to help one another feel the value of these experiences while they are happening, if we can; this also holds true for any disappointment or suffering in the experience of normal human living." [29]

FAITH AND HEALING

The relation of religious faith to physical healing is an area of rapidly increasing exploration. With so much popular interest, the way is open for demagogues and charlatans.

Today one of the greatest needs the church can fill is to the sick and suffering people in our hospitals. This is a relatively new field of service; a pioneer area for Christian ministry. A hospital chaplain writes:

"The presence of the chaplain at the bedside of the sick brings a message of strength and comfort in the realm beyond speech, as well as through words suited to the particular needs of the patient. The chaplain not only ministers directly to the patient, but his (or her) influence is also channeled indirectly through his (or her) association and work with the hospital's medical and office staff. The chaplain is one of a three-member healing-team: the doctor, the nurse, and the chaplain.

"The Christian ministry of the hospital chaplain teaches the sick to use their suffering to find new meaning in life. If the church does not arise to this need, it will miss what might well be one of its greatest opportunities to help the ill into increased spiritual awareness and growth. The hospital with a chaplain can bring healing to the whole person—to his suffering body, his mind, and his spirit." [30]

In his very helpful book, *Faith Healing and the Christian Faith,* Wade H. Boggs, Jr., has made a thorough study of the healing miracles of Jesus.* He points out that there are forty-one specific instances of Jesus' healing power recorded in the New Testament, of which thirty-three or possibly thirty-four refer to the cure of physical infirmities. Of these, nineteen or twenty are described with sufficient clarity for them to be studied in detail.

These cures performed by the Christ have occasioned much study and many books.

First, why did Jesus heal?

As to why Christ healed, Dr. Boggs states that there are those who hold that Jesus performed his amazing works of healing in order to arouse public interest and win acceptance of his gospel. The cures drew crowds. They also served to accredit Christ's message.

When John the Baptist was languishing in prison, he seemed to have some doubts as to whether this Nazarene carpenter whom he had baptized was the true Messiah. He sent messengers to Jesus, saying, "Are you he who is to come, or shall we look for another?" Jesus answered the messengers, saying, "Go and tell John what you have seen and heard: the blind receive their sight, the lame walk, lepers are cleansed, and the deaf hear, the dead are raised up, the poor have good news preached to them" (Luke 7:20, 22-23).

Though this might seem to indicate that Jesus cited his cures as evidence of his messiahship and the truth of his message, there is overwhelming evidence that he sought to subordinate his healing work to the proclaiming of the gospel, to make the cure of the body secondary to the healing of the soul. Repeatedly he

---

*Note: I wish to express special indebtedness for material on these pages quoted directly and indirectly from "Do New Testament Miracles Still Occur?" Chapter IV of Dr. Boggs' book.

bade those whom he had healed not to publicize the cure.

Recall the ruler of the synagogue whose little daughter was supposedly dead. Jesus went to his house allowing no one to follow him except Peter, James, and John. When he came to the house, he put them all outside and took the child's father and mother and went in where the child was. Taking the child by the hand, he said, "Little girl, I say to you arise". (Mark 5:41). And immediately the little girl stood up and walked. And Jesus "strictly charged them that no one should know this" (Mark 5:43).

Such references, which could be multiplied, reveal how different Jesus' methods of healing were from the highly publicized, widely televised methods of some modern faith healers. (Jesus seemed to fear that the reports of his miraculous cures would confuse people as to his true mission and keep them from understanding his major emphasis on moral conformity to the will of God.) Jesus refused to perform cures just to satisfy the curiosity of his critics. He knew that spectacular cures would not convert the souls of the impenitent.

In his parable of Dives and Lazarus, Jesus represents Dives as dead and in torment, asking Abraham to send Lazarus to warn his brothers lest they follow after him to Hades. But Abraham answered him, saying, "If they do not hear Moses and the prophets, neither will they be convinced if someone should rise from the dead" (Luke 16:31).

No, it was not to dazzle the crowds with spectacular demonstrations of miraculous power that Jesus healed, but to reveal to them, and to all men, God's infinite compassion. He knew that men's hearts could not be changed by "signs" and wonders, but only by the realization that God was a God of mercy and love.

Compassion lay at the heart of his healing. Again and again we read how Jesus was "moved with compassion," a compassion that lay deeper than pity for the sufferings inflicted by an ailing body. The Gospels make it clear that he healed not merely to make a person physically fit, but to "restore the physical, mental and spiritual harmony of the whole personality of the sufferer by placing him in a new and right relation to God, to his neighbor and to himself."

Consider the case of the leper of whom Mark tells in his first chapter. When the leper knelt before Jesus, asking to be made clean, Jesus touched him. Since lepers were shunned, this act helped to restore the poor victim's faith in human brotherhood. Then Jesus added, "Go, show yourself to the priest, and offer for cleansing what Moses commanded, for a proof to the people" (Mark 1:44). The priests alone had authority to pronounce a leper cleansed and therefore fit again for normal human relationships.

How did Jesus heal?

A reading of the Gospels reveals how Jesus varied his methods to suit the needs of his patients. This, too, is described by Dr. Boggs. Eight of Jesus' cures were performed on persons who "seemed to have some sort of faith prior to the cure." For instance, he said to the ruler of the synagogue whose daughter was considered dead, "Do not fear, only believe" (Luke 8:50). When the two blind men asked him to restore their sight, Jesus said, "Do you believe that I am able to do this?" (Matt. 9:28). And when they replied, "Yes, Lord," he healed them, saying, "According to your faith be it done to you." To the leper who returned to thank him for his cleansing, Christ said, "Go your way: your faith has made you well" (Luke 17:19).

We can understand how a patient's faith helps in

the healing process. But there are three cases where cures were effected, not by the faith of the sick, but by that of relatives and friends.

When the crowd in Capernaum was so dense that the people could not get into the house to reach Jesus, four men carried a paralytic and let him down through the roof. The record is that when Jesus saw *"their faith,"* he proceeded to heal the patient. In another instance Jesus marvelled at the faith of a Roman centurion which was instrumental in healing his slave. "I have not found so great faith," he exclaimed, "no not in Israel!"

While we cannot fully comprehend the way the faith of other persons helps in healing a patient, we are prepared to believe that the "psychic atmosphere created by numerous persons of faith who pray for the sick person can release divine healing powers which otherwise might be blocked by indifference or ill will." The Gospels record that in certain places Christ could not do mighty works of healing because of the popular unbelief.

In his healing work Christ used not only cooperating faith, but also the power of suggestion. "For example, on several occasions Jesus used saliva in connection with his cures. It was believed in New Testament days that saliva had curative powers. . . ." When Jesus beheld the man who was born blind, he "spat on the ground and made clay of the spittle and anointed the man's eyes with the clay," and told him to go wash in the pool of Siloam (John 9:6-7). "Jesus' use of spittle was not magical but suggestive. Thus Jesus was acting out what He proposed to do in such a way that these persons might understand it and be aroused into an attitude of trustful expectancy; He was reinforcing the power of suggestion by the use of a physical measure generally accepted in that day as efficacious."

Also, Jesus sometimes laid his hands on the sick. Again this act, while not directly necessary to the process of healing, carried with it the value of suggestion, since it was a technique used by ancient healers, and hence was familiar to the people.

But let us be clear: Jesus did not heal merely by suggestion. "He sought to bring into existence a life-giving relationship to God, which would have its effect upon the habit pattern of the patient, thus releasing healing powers, and tending to prevent recurrence of the disease."

There are at least two cases in which Jesus healed sicknesses that were due to sin. Consider the paralytic who was let down through the roof by his friends. Jesus said to him, "My son, your sins are forgiven" (Matt. 9:2).

The connection between guilt-consciousness and physical illness has been repeatedly observed. Ministers and physicians today have noted an amazing variety of disorders which have been relieved and even cured by bringing the patient into healing contact with the mercy of God. Forgiveness opens the way for a new life resulting from a restored fellowship with God.

Dr. Boggs's study of Christ's cures therefore leads him to the conclusion that they were not "magical, capricious displays of power, but illustrations of law-abiding methods of healing, which we are at least beginning to comprehend" today. We call them miracles, but a miracle is an act of God which outruns our reason but does not outrage our reason. It is not a violation of natural law but a manifestation of law which we have not yet fathomed. Miracles may be departures from God's habitual ways of acting, but we cannot say that they contradict God's nature. What we call the laws of nature are merely man-made constructions resulting from our observance of nature's routine methods. As human knowledge has increased, many things once regarded as miracles are no longer so interpreted. As Dr. J. D. Van Buskirk, the distinguished missionary doctor, says: "Our glimpses into scientific laws and our expanding knowledge give us ever increasing power to do things that are more like His marvelous works." [31]

Yet this ever increasing power falls short of that of our Lord since, as the author of *Faith Healing and Christian Faith* reminds us, "He [Jesus] was a unique person. His relation to God was unique.... He differed from us in that there was perfect concord and harmony in all aspects of His Being, in that He was perfectly submissive to the will of God, and in that His relationship to other people was always based on perfect love. As a result of all this, He possessed greater spiritual energy and deeper spiritual insight than we can ever hope to achieve." [32]

In the light of Jesus' purpose and methods of healing, how are we to relate our Christian faith to our own health?

For one thing, we are to recognize all healing as divine healing. Some years ago a popular faith healer declared, "If you can't trust the Lord, then call the doctor." Such a statement is based on a mistaken concept of scriptural teaching.

Jesus recognized the work of the physician when he said to the Pharisee, "Those who are well have no need of a physician, but those who are sick" (Matt. 9:12).

Or recall the time when King Hezekiah was sick and the prophet Isaiah told him he would soon die. And Hezekiah prayed a prayer of repentance. As Isaiah was leaving the king's court he received a message from the

Lord saying, "Go and say to Hezekiah, 'Thus says the Lord. . . . I have heard your prayer, . . . behold I will add fifteen years to your life' " (Isa. 38:5).

The prophet Isaiah returned to Hezekiah's court, but he said to the king's servants, "Let them take a cake of figs, and apply it to the boil, that he may recover" (Isa. 38:21). The prophet had faith in God's healing power but he also used the best medical aid he knew. Ezekiel in his prophecy refers to the use of appliances for containing fractures. St. Paul chose as his companion on two of his missionary journeys Luke, a doctor, and refers to him as "the beloved physician" (Col. 4:14).

On numerous occasions the scriptural writers refer approvingly to the use of oil for medicinal purposes. Jesus, in the parable of the Good Samaritan, told how the kindly rescuer, after binding up the robbed man's wounds, poured oil and wine to soften the wound. The instruction of Jesus to the disciples to anoint with oil and heal the sick led to widespread use of oil by Christians in healing. In the light of all this, we can say that the physician has the sanction of Scriptures for his calling.

On the other hand, the good doctor recognizes that his skill and his medicines serve to clear away the barriers so that God's healing power may do its work. Over the entrance to the Presbyterian Hospital in New York City are carved in stone these words: "For of the Most High cometh healing."

A Christian physician once said, concerning his patient, "I tended him; God healed him." Ben Franklin, with his practical philosophy, asserted that God helps those who help themselves. Yet, while he would have men use every means they knew, Benjamin Franklin recognized that the healing force is from God and said humorously, "God heals and the doctor takes the fee." (The humor of Franklin's remark does not dull the truth that God works through the doctor just as truly as through faith and prayer.)

A second thing we can say is that we can use our Christian faith to aid the healing process. We can agree with the faith healers that we should have more faith. But Christian faith is not credulity. It is not blind belief which runs counter to reason. Faith is guided by reason. We ought to have faith in those promises or positions which have the most evidence to support them.

Yet the universe is so complex that our finite minds can apprehend only a small fraction of the factors which play on any situation. Hence we have to live by the force of faith. We have to trust beyond that we can see or know.

Our Christian faith holds that this universe can best be explained as the creation of an Almighty God whose fatherly nature is revealed in the life and love of Jesus Christ. Resting in this undergirding faith, we confront all problems, including that of sickness. In whatever happens, we have faith that God is working for our best interests. This kind of trust helps to change the mental outlook in ways that aid the healing process. Mental depression gives way to optimism; the defeatist spirit is lifted to new hope; the weary mind finds new strength; the burden of guilt is removed by the assurance of forgiveness—all this is of immeasurable aid in opening the way for God's healing work in our bodies. And even if our illness is not cured, we discover with St. Paul, when his thorn remained, that grace is given sufficient to bear it.

And our Christian faith does a third thing for us. It keeps us ever mindful that God's will for us is to make us Christlike in character. We are to grow up into Christ who is the head of the body (the church); that we may "attain to . . . the measure of the stature of the fullness of Christ" (Eph. 4:13).

Health of body is, therefore, subordinate to health of spirit. Our primary purpose is not to use God to keep ourselves physically fit, but to use our bodies in order to be spiritually fit. (Sometimes our bodily pains help to produce spiritual health.) After Paul repeatedly prayed for the cure of his thorn in the flesh, he heard the Lord say to him, "My grace is sufficient for you, for my power is made perfect in weakness" (II Cor. 12:9).

About five years ago, just before Christmas, a noble Presbyterian minister, Dr. Edmund Wylie, passed away. His Christmas card was received by his friends after his fatal cerebral hemorrhage. Its message read: "There is a faith greater than that of answered prayer; that is the faith of the man on the cross who was born at Christmas . . . that great faith, I wish for you."

CHAPTER IV

The Values of Suffering

DISCIPLINE

Some years ago Aldous Huxley in his book, *Brave New World,* pictured a land from which all harsh and painful features had been removed. The Controller of it proudly declared, "It is Christianity without tears." "But," cried another voice, "the tears are necessary. You get rid of them. You just abolish the slings and arrows. It's too easy. I don't want comfort. I want God. I want poetry. I want real danger. I want freedom."

> The Controller replied,
> "But you'll be very unhappy."
> The other retorted:
> "I claim the right to be unhappy." [33]

A little second-thought reveals that a world without hardships would be unendurable. Without the warning of pain our bodies would not preserve their health. Without danger there would be no adventure. Without friction our cars would not start and our spirits would not soar. Without tears, eyes would not shine with their richest expressions.

Some time ago I was in an upstate New York city. It was a bitterly cold night, ten below zero and the roads were icy. My host's son and his fiancée had driven over from Cornell some thirty miles away. Before they started back, my host went down to the furnace room and brought a bucket of ashes to put in their car, so that, if they got stuck on the slippery road, the ashes would give the tires some grip. Similarly the ashes of suffering have to be carried on the journey of life so that faith and hope and love can keep going.

When we protestingly ask, "Why does a good God permit pain and evil in the world?" one answer could be that he does it for the good of his children. And it could even be added that, without some hardships and dangers and trouble, life would not seem good to us.

This is the truth which the Epistle to the Hebrews is stressing in its twelfth chapter. The writer reminds his readers that "God disciplines him whom he loves" for he is thus treating the person as a son. (Our earthly parents discipline us and we respect them. Shall we not much more respect the discipline of our heavenly Father who does it for our own good?) We may not appreciate God's purpose at the time and we may resent it. "For the moment all discipline seems painful rather than pleasant: later it yields the peaceful fruit of righteousness to those who have been trained by it" (Heb. 12:11).

We should say at the outset, as we have in preceding pages, that not all pain and trouble are to be looked upon as God's discipline. Mystery enshrouds the causes of much suffering. Many of our troubles are brought on by our carelessness, our cruelty, our misuse of freedom. The tragic crash of a plane with the loss of many lives can by no stretch of the imagination be interpreted as God's way of disciplining the individuals or the company involved. The polio germ which cripples your little daughter is not sent by God to teach her patience. And when nations drift into war, it is heinous impiety to say that it is God's will and that the massacre of millions is God's method of disciplining his wayward children.

God's universe is too vast for us to comprehend all

the causes of our sufferings. God's love is too deep for us to discern all his purposes. God's Fatherhood is such that he has to give his children freedom to grow and thereby they bring on some pains which he does not intend or desire. But if we grasp the fact of God's Fatherhood, we come to see some of our hardships as his discipline. There are some pains in life which God uses for our good.

For one thing, God disciplines us to make us more teachable. Oliver Wendell Holmes in *The Poet at the Breakfast Table* said that there are some people who seem to have no bent for religion just as there are persons who have no ear for music. He admitted that he was one who did not take naturally to religion, but he was turned to it "by the discipline of trials in the life of outward circumstance" he had to endure. "It was needful that I should learn the meaning of that text, 'Whom the Lord loveth he chasteneth,' " [34] he wrote.

Life may move along so smoothly that we feel self-sufficient. Never feeling the need for higher help, we immerse ourselves in the secular things around us. We leave God out of the picture and seem to get along pretty well without him, until adversity or emergency sets us groping for something beyond ourselves.

John Buchan, late governor general of Canada, once said that religion is born when we accept the ultimate frustration of mere human effort, and at the same time realize the strength which comes from union with superhuman reality.

Consider the case of Moses. Reared in the royal court of the Pharaohs, Moses could naturally expect to grow up in Egyptian luxury. But he remained loyal to his Hebrew countrymen. One day he saw an Egyptian beating an Israelite. In impulsive anger Moses slew the Egyptian and buried his body in the sand. The next day Moses was walking along the road and he saw two of his Hebrew countrymen in a quarrel. When he remonstrated with "the man that did the wrong," he cried, "Do you mean to kill me as you killed the Egyptian?" (Ex. 2:14). Thereupon Moses knew that his deed of anger had been discovered. Also, he felt that his own fellow Hebrews were not grateful for what he had done for them. Hence in dejection and bitterness of spirit Moses left Egypt and became a herder of flocks in Midian.

But later, out on the range in Midian, Moses had an experience at the burning bush—the bush seemed to burn and yet was not consumed. He felt confronted by the Lord himself. And he heard the Lord saying to him: "I am the God of your father, the God of Abraham, the God of Isaac, and the God of Jacob" (Ex. 3:6). Then God told him to go back to Egypt and redeem his people. From dwelling dismally on his own defects, Moses' depressed spirit was uplifted to receive divine inspiration and guidance. He who had withdrawn from those who needed him was sent back to become their leader in the mighty exodus from Egypt. The hot temper which had gotten him into trouble as a young man became so disciplined that he led his countrymen for forty years through countless irritations on that gruelling trek across the wilderness toward Canaan. And the secret of his patient and persevering leadership is given in Scripture thus: "He endured as seeing him who is invisible" (Heb. 11:27).

Others might have had those early trials and frustrations of Moses without being disciplined by them. It does not follow that defeat and tribulation always develop teachable minds. For instance, we may trust ourselves to a person and he deceive us. We say, "I am wise to him," which means that our faith has been lessened to some extent. Or we give ourselves to a project and it turns out badly. We say, "I burned my fingers once, but never again." Hands with burned fingers are less prone to grasp other hands in trust. Thus defeats and failures and sufferings may leave us with burned fingers and cold shoulders which cause our faith and fellowship to shrink.

If we are to get wisdom and strength rather than cynicism and weakness from our adversities, we must be rooted in the belief that God disciplines those whom he loves. The same sun and warmth which cause the flower in the ground to grow will wither the flower that is cut off from the earth. When Harry Lauder, the Scottish singer and comedian, lost his son during World War I, he is reported as having said to a friend that at such a time a man can do one of three things: turn to drink, to despair, or to God.[35] Harry Lauder turned to God, and God turned his tragedy into a triumph of the spirit.

Trouble does not always open our hearts and minds to God. Here is a test to think about. When painful misfortune comes, does it humble us or merely humiliate us? If we are centered in self, then trouble only makes us feel humiliated. We think of how we look in the eyes of others, how we are pitied or shamed. But if we are really God-centered rather than self-centered, then trouble serves to humble us and make us more teachable.

Growth

Bodily pain serves as a warning to further our physical growth and preserve our health. With all the best of protection, what child can grow up without risking the pain of falling? How would a child learn to walk without some falls? If there is any absolutely painless way of rearing children, grandparents would have surely discovered it!

Also, growing up involves a certain amount of outgrowing. And outgrowing often involves the strain of pressure, the struggle of separation, perhaps the suffering of loneliness. There are times when it hurts to grow. Nowhere is this truth so vividly revealed as in the life of Jesus himself.

In the Epistle to the Hebrews, written after his crucifixion, the fifth chapter records these words: "Although he was a Son, he learned obedience through what he suffered" (5:8). From this reference we infer that our Lord entered so fully into the limitations of human life that he experienced processes of growth and the hurts incident thereto.

Consider first the circle of family relationship. Luke lifts the curtain to give us one view of Jesus as a growing boy. When he was twelve his parents took him to the temple at Jerusalem for the Feast of the Passover. On their homeward journey Joseph and Mary missed the lad and became anxious. They finally found him in the Temple discussing questions with the teachers of the law. Mary said to him: "Son, why have you treated us so? Behold, your father and I have been looking for you anxiously." Jesus loved his parents devotedly and it must have hurt his sensitive loving nature to reply: "Do you not know that I must be in my Father's house?" (Luke 2:48-49). Jesus was growing beyond his parents' understanding.

There are times when tension between parents and children can be termed growing pains. Perhaps such times are comparatively rare. More usually the strain within the family is due to the fact that the children are not growing up to their parents, rather than to the fact that they are outgrowing them. The old commandment, "Honor thy father and thy mother," is still imperatively needed. The willful child who wants his own way for his own pleasure, the sophisticated youth who thinks his parents are old-fashioned because they do not approve all the new-fangled extreme practices of youth—these are not growing beyond their parents.

A child's nature is like a garden. We may plough and harrow the ground so that it looks absolutely clean. There is not a visible sign of any growing thing. But that clean brown earth has seeds in it remaining from previous growths. And if it is left untended, absolutely free from disturbance, it will bring forth perhaps some flowers from last season's growth, and also most assuredly it will bring forth some weeds. So with the child. Just let it grow, free and untended, and it will show the weeds of evil as well as the flowers of virtue. Therefore, the child needs, as we say in the baptismal ritual, "the restraining and renewing influence" of God's spirit.

When we think of the problems faced by today's youth, we feel increased sympathy for both them and their parents. Not only is discipline more difficult, but understanding becomes more difficult because the speed of change is so much faster and the pressure so much greater. It takes more study and stronger character to cultivate wholesome family life in 1961 than in 1900. A North Carolina Supervisor of Public School Teachers declared a year or so ago: "The worst thing that could happen to our world would be for our children to grow up to be like us." They must have larger visions and sturdier standards than ours.

And parents should remember that they can learn from their children as well as teach them. The child sometimes has a purity of mind and freshness of insight which parents need to get. Is that not why Jesus once set a child in the midst of some grownups and said:

"Unless you turn and become like children, you will never enter the kingdom of heaven" (Matt. 18:3)?

Sometimes a high sense of duty drives a son or daughter, as it drove Jesus, to go beyond the family pattern and thus cause pain. I think of a young woman in my boyhood community who felt called to be a foreign missionary. In those days it was felt in her rural section that to go to the foreign mission field was like dropping off the earth. The parents grieved deeply at the thought of her leaving them. But duty called her, and later her family forgot the pain in their joy over her great service.

A little over fifty years ago a sixteen-year-old youth in Japan joined an English Bible class taught by an American missionary. The boy came from a family background of wealth and social standing. His uncle was heading him toward diplomacy. But the atmosphere of the home was unspiritual and the boy was restless. He became imbued with the spirit of Christ and began to serve a Christian Sunday school. His uncle disinherited him and he went penniless to a theological seminary. He began to preach and teach in a slum district. That youth was Kagawa, later to become the most outstanding Christian leader in Japan. Like his Lord, Kagawa learned obedience by what he suffered. It hurt him to grow up, but he grew.[36]

Jesus in his family relations suffered and caused pain, not only in the Temple at the age of twelve but later in the pursuit of his ministry. His family wanted to protect him from the dangers into which his course was leading him. They saw the rising opposition against him and, on one occasion, went to call him back from his perilous mission. Word was sent to Jesus where he was speaking that his mother and brothers were outside calling for him. Jesus cried: " 'Who is my mother, and who are my brothers?' And stretching out his hand toward his disciples, he said, 'Here are my mother and my brothers. For whoever does the will of my Father in heaven is my brother, and sister, and mother'" (Matt. 12:48-50). It must certainly have cost Jesus pain to utter these words. But he was showing that at times the call of God transcends the call of family.

Let us turn from the family circle to the *community* and consider a second situation where it often hurts to grow. After Jesus' baptism and his temptation in the wilderness, he spent a brief time healing and teaching around Capernaum. Then he returned to his home town of Nazareth. I believe that Jesus was sufficiently human to feel what a young man feels about his home town. A young man likes to be thought well of by his neighbors. He dreams of coming back with honor and respect.

As his custom was, Jesus went into the synagogue on the Sabbath. They asked him to read. He opened the Scripture to the words of Isaiah the prophet:

> "The Spirit of the Lord is upon me,
>   because he has anointed me to preach good news
>   to the poor,
>   He has sent me to proclaim release to the captives
>   and recovering of sight to the blind,
>   to set at liberty those who are oppressed,
>   to proclaim the acceptable year of the Lord."

As he closed the book, Jesus said to his hearers: "Today this scripture has been fulfilled in your hearing" (Luke 4:18-19, 21).

These words astounded his neighbors. Jesus was asserting that he was the anointed of God. His hearers were impressed by his words, and whispered among themselves. They said, "Is not this Joseph's son?" They were probably thinking that if he could demonstrate his divine power by doing some wonderful works he would put Nazareth on the map. Jesus, divining their thoughts, said: "Doubtless you will quote to me this proverb, 'Physician, heal yourself'; what we have heard you did at Capernaum, do here also in your own country" (Luke 4:23). Surely if Jesus could heal at Capernaum, he should do even more mighty works in his home town. Charity begins at home. And a prophet's first duty is to his own neighborhood.

But Jesus went on to cite the case of the prophet Elijah who appeared at a time of great drought and famine. Yet Elijah went out from his home region to help a poor widow in the land of Sidon. And also he mentioned how the prophet Elisha went forth to heal, not the lepers of his own Israel, but a Syrian named Naaman.

These words of Jesus were not pleasing to his Nazarene neighbors, and it certainly must have hurt Jesus to utter them. But he had to break through the narrowness and self-centeredness of his own community.

Jesus was trying to teach them that they could be saved only by going out from themselves, as did Elijah and Elisha. That was not popular preaching then. Nor is it so now. What we like to hear is how to get things from God for ourselves. The preacher who can show what prayer can do for us is popular. The church that can show that it increases the social and property values of the community is supported. But when a prophetic preacher runs counter to the mores of a community and tries to arouse people from their smug complacency, and set them to unselfish service, then he encounters trouble and is likely to incur pain. In the case of Jesus, the record is that his Nazarene neighbors rose up and put him out of the city, even threatening to throw him over the brow of the hill.

Loyalty to community, like loyalty to family, is one

of our noblest sentiments. It helps to form the strength of a nation. I have often said that the spirit of community is our best defense against communism. Let a resident feel that he is accepted by a community, that he belongs to its social and religious life, and he is pretty immune to communist infection.

But in our community life there is the danger of too great conformity to its patterns. President Claude Bissell warned his students at Toronto University against too much emphasis on teaching that they should be "well adjusted." It is not the aim of the university, he said, to produce "dumplings." [37] No one wants to be called a dumpling, and no one wants to look like a dumpling. But there is an ominous trend in that direction. The London *Times Literary Supplement*, a few years ago, described the younger generation as "possessing an excess of moderation," and a "hostility to sublime mysticism." And Professor Wallace Stegner of Stanford University, writing in *The Nation*, said that the undergraduate shuns causes, heroes, joinings, commitments.

But the person who grows up with Christ is not content to be well adjusted to things as they are in his community. He feels called upon to obey God rather than men.

About 750 years ago a young lad grew up in an Italian village. His father was a rich merchant and wanted his son to carry on the business. But after a short while the young man became convinced that he should try to follow as nearly as possible the example of Jesus. He went forth as a penniless worker to help the lepers and outcasts. It was in the period when the church was building magnificent cathedrals and sending mighty crusades across Europe to free Palestine from the Turks. The devout were looking for God in big spectacular things and this frail little friar seemed a pitiful figure. They looked condescendingly upon him because of his association with the lepers, and they laughed at his idea of cultivating friendship with the Turks. But that friar who broke through the patterns of his family and his community was Francis of Assisi, who is now remembered as Saint Francis, the most radiant figure of the Dark Ages.

Let us go on a third step to consider how it hurt Jesus to grow in the circle of his own followers. Observe him at Caesarea Philippi. Jesus was at the peak of his popularity. Great crowds were following him. He had just fed the multitudes. Simon Peter had made his great confession, hailing Jesus as "the Christ, the Son of the living God" (Matt. 16:16). It seemed as if Jesus could go on indefinitely with mounting acclaim.

Then Matthew records: "From that time Jesus began to show his disciples that he must go to Jerusalem and suffer many things" (Matt. 16:21), even death itself. Immediately Peter began to rebuke Jesus, saying, "God forbid, Lord! This shall never happen to you." But the Master turned to Peter and said: "Get behind me, Satan! You are a hindrance to me, for you are not on the side of God, but of men" (Matt. 16:22-23).

It certainly must have hurt Jesus to say those words to Peter. He knew that Peter's protest was prompted by his desire to protect him. But Christ's suffering at that moment was a growing pain, for he had to go beyond even the desires of his disciples. He had to show that the heart of the gospel is in the cross.

Think how it hurt Paul to grow out of his secure Jewish social setting to join the new sect of the Christians. Think how it hurt him again to go against Peter and James, his new colleagues in carrying the gospel to the Gentiles.

And think how it hurt John Wesley, the polished and conservative priest in the Church of England, to go out and preach on the streets and be scorned by his former fellow churchmen.

(To grow up in Christ will bring pain, for you will have to outgrow some of the conventions of comfortable churchmanship, some of the customs of your social circles, some of the frontiers of your business systems. But you will be following One who said, "Be of good cheer, I have overcome the world") (John 16:33).

Resourcefulness

If we were always bland, always placidly confident, always smilingly untroubled; if there were no shadows of untoward circumstance, no dark nights of the soul when we toss sleeplessly on our beds seeking the light until the pupils of our mental eyes widen; if our world contained no pain to prick our ease, no suffering to call forth our compassion, no inexplicable sorrows to accept in faith and love; if our days were all sunshine—our lives would become a desert, our streams of sympathy would dry up, our eyes would become spiritually blind and our natures swinishly selfish.

It is against dark velvet that diamonds are displayed to show their lustre. It is in the darkness that we discover the deeper meanings and richer resources of life.

Consider the qualities of character which make it noble and strong. How do they come? Think of patience which is developed when we have to stand and wait, when we must walk and not faint, when we cannot do anything but stand and take it. Or consider fortitude, which is courage refined in the fire of endurance. Or think of kindness and compassion. Only those who have been hurt know how to help without hurting.

We might live only for the present, as the lower animals do, if our imaginations did not disturb us with the thought of future frustration and hardship. A wise administrator once said that every man is as lazy as he dares to be, and that the only difference which makes some of us work harder is that we are gifted with imagination to look farther ahead and see the doom catching up with us. There is enough truth in that statement to make us analyze our motives. We tend to settle down in easy nests, but then we are troubled by the painful thought of how such an easy life will handicap us in the years ahead.

Or it may be that the pain of present circumstances spurs us to plan for the future. Booker T. Washington once spoke of "the advantage of disadvantages." And certainly he ought to have known what he was talking about. Born a slave, he carried the books of his white master's children to school, but *his* schooling he had to get the hard way. He knew the early defeats of the spirit. Yet out of it he got such a passion for education, and such a desire to serve his own race, that his career became an inspiration to all races.

Or, consider how our native abilities need painful prodding to awaken us to our larger responsibilities. Beethoven said of Rossini that he had in him the making of a great musician, which he could have become if he had only been well flogged as a boy, but that he had been spoiled by his facility for composition. However true or false Beethoven's appraisal of Rossini, it is a fact that early success and self-assurance have often not been tempered by sufficient hardship and struggle to develop great talent.

Quite in line with Beethoven's remark was that of a Viennese music teacher in regard to one of his own pupils. He said: "She is a magnificent singer, and yet there's just something lacking in her singing. Life has been too kind to her. But if one day it happened that some one broke her heart, she would be the finest singer in Europe!" [38]

We cannot interpret the deep and tender emotions of life until we have experienced them. And we cannot realize the full rich life until we have been tested in the refiner's fire of suffering. Some years ago Edna Ferber in her book, *So Big*, depicted a rugged, vital woman who, through hardship and struggle, achieved a commanding career. She had a son who basked in the sunshine of his mother's financial success. He was sent to the best schools, given strategic opportunities, protected from the harsh actualities of life. He grew up a polished, urbane, ineffectual person. Sizing him up one day his mother said to him: "You are just too smooth." No wrinkles in his face marked the strain of struggle. No strong sinews of mind and no deep emotions of heart were developed in him.

John Ruskin in his *Seven Lamps of Architecture* asserted that the power of architecture is measured in part by the quantity of its shadow. A building, such as a church, should express a kind of human sympathy by a measure of darkness as great as there is in human life. And great living is marked by shadow. Can you think of any great character who never suffered at least one defeat? Do you know of any really big heart that has never been broken at least once? Would Dante have discovered the depths of his own heart and the height of his own genius had it not been for Beatrice and the vicissitudes of their love? It was not until his heart was surcharged with personal suffering and public sorrow that he wrote his *Divine Comedy*. It was in the shadow of threatening death that Mozart composed his immortal *Requiem*.

Consider also how God develops greater resourcefulness in us through the discipline of limitations. When illness or frustration limits us, we can with God's help make better use of the strength we have left. (When our resources seem unlimited, we are so prone to be wasteful.) Youth in the glow of exuberant health assumes its energy is boundless and often proceeds to "burn the candle at both ends," thus depleting the energy needed for future endurance. But when something happens to show us that time and strength are limited, God teaches us "to number our days that we may get a heart of wisdom" (Psalm 90:12).

Can we take the remaining fraction of life and make it radiant? Paul said: "When I am weak, then I am strong" (II Cor. 12:10). He remained "steadfast, immovable, always abounding in the work of the Lord," because he knew that his labor was not in vain in the Lord (I Cor. 15:58).

Dr. Leslie Weatherhead of London has a favorite figure to illustrate this principle of development through loss or pain. It is the parallel of the making of a Persian rug. In weaving a Persian rug, the rug is hung vertically on a frame and boys are posted in the rear of it at different levels. The designer stands out in front and calls to the boys to pull certain threads. Sometimes the boys make mistakes.

Dr. Weatherhead says that he has a Persian rug given him by an Arab sheik which has a yellow irregularity in it. But he prizes this irregularity as evidence of the rug's value. It shows it was not made by a machine in an English carpet factory. Once he had the opportunity to ask a young Persian studying in England, "What happens when the boy makes a mistake?" "Well," said the student, "quite often the artist does not make the little boy take out the wrong color. If he is a great enough artist, he weaves the mistake into the pattern."

Weatherhead uses that illustration as a parable of the loss or pain that comes to us by reason of our mistakes. "Evil is evil and loss is loss," he writes, "but God has the power, out of and through the evil and the loss, to bring good and gain." [39]

The Master somehow can make it all work together for good. With God's help we can take the pain, the mistakes, the disease, and weave them into a richer character.

Dr. James Stewart of Edinburgh has pointed out an interesting thing. The word "strain" has two meanings. It can mean "stress, suffering, or trouble." But it can also mean a strain of music, "song." He thinks there is a significance in this and quotes Ernest Raymond as saying that the world's greatest literature has sprung from "the hurt of highly sensitized souls." [40] "Our sweetest songs are those which tell of saddest thought," says Shelley in his ode "To a Skylark." The ability to take the stress and strain of life and make them into strains of music constitutes great living.

We frequently cite the case of Robert Louis Stevenson as an example of gallant living. Let me quote something that Stevenson wrote: "For fourteen years I have had not a day's real health; I have wakened sick and gone to bed weary; and I have done my day unflinchingly. I have written in bed, and written out of it, written in hemorrhages, written in sickness, written torn by coughing, written when my head swam from weakness; and for so long, it seems to me I have won my wager and recovered my glove. . . . At least I have not failed, but I would have preferred a place of trumpetings, and the open air over my head. . . . And the battle goes on—ill or well, is a trifle, so as it goes. I was made for a contest, and the Powers have so willed that my battle-field should be this dingy, inglorious one of the bed and the physic bottle." [41] And yet those who knew Robert Louis Stevenson found him a brave, gay minstrel of the spirit. He had found the profit in pain, because he learned, from what he suffered, the principles of rich personality.

It often seems that there is a link of causal connection between physical suffering and the highest creative work .The annals of literature reveal a remarkable story. Think of Milton's blindness, Alexander Pope's grotesque deformity, the tubercular Keats and Emily Brontë; think of Emerson and Tennyson with their chronic infections, the epilepsy of Swinburne and Flaubert, the neuralgia of Dickens and Gamaliel Bradford. There is hardly a sound body in the roster of the world's most distinguished writers; and of those blessed with physical health, there was nearly always a spiritual anguish that had to be borne. Even the healthy Goethe once said: "I never had an affliction that I did not turn into a poem." And the poet Heine, who suffered much both physically and mentally, wrote

> Out of my deepest sorrows,
> I make my little songs.

UNDERSTANDING

Some years ago I knew a man who was so continuously successful that he was a marvel to all his acquaintances. Possessed of an attractive personality, he was a supersalesman who could turn almost anything he touched into gold. In fact, so unbroken were his success and advancement that he could not easily understand those who failed or lost out in the financial race.

Then reverses came to him. Through the mismanagement of a man he trusted, his family savings were swept away. His health broke for a time. But out of it all he developed a more sympathetic understanding of others, a more winsome attitude toward youth, a deeper dependence on God. He became one of the most engaging and effective Christian laymen I have ever known.

A break in the family circle, for instance, brings its pang of loneliness, but it may also serve to remind us of the love which flowed so steadily through the household that it was taken for granted without gratitude. A break in business brings hardship, but it may also throw fresh light on the favorable factors which continue and may raise the question of making a living into the larger issue of making a life. A break in health brings pain, but while it takes the patient out of the stream of activity for a time, it may show him what the real current of life is, as distinguished from its eddies. How often it happens that it takes an interruption to reveal the continuity.

One of the great secrets of victorious living is to see through the breaks in life to the things which abide, to see through a wife's momentary flash of anger to her enduring love, to see through the treachery of one false friend to the loyalty of countless others; (to hold on, as Elijah did, through the earthquake and storm, until the still small voice is heard.) Hear the words of one who had mastered this secret as he says: "Who shall separate us from the love of Christ? Shall tribulation, or distress, or persecution, or famine, or nakedness, or peril, or sword? . . . No, in all these things we are more than conquerors through him who loved us" (Rom. 8:35-37). There speaks one who saw through the changes in life to the things that last.

A second way in which we may see God at the turns comes when changes spiritualize the current of life. The tendency of daily living is toward material things. Our physical concerns are ever to the fore. Our five senses keep us occupied with the securing of their satisfactions. Amid all our engagements with the things that are seen and temporal, we take little time for the things that are unseen and eternal.

Dr. Olin Stockwell, the distinguished missionary, was imprisoned in Communist China for more than two and a half years. There he endured the cruelty of "brainwashing." But his book, *With God in Red China*, reveals the enriching insights which came to him in prison—as they came to John Bunyan who glimpsed the gates of the Celestial City through the bars of Bedford jail.

Paralleling these Christian experiences are the words of Sakini in the *Teahouse of the August Moon*. After the various vicissitudes of the rise and fall of the teahouse, Sakini sagely says: "Suffering makes men think, thinking makes them wise, and wisdom makes the world endurable." [42]

Yes, more than endurable if the suffering is endured with patient fortitude and for a noble purpose. In the overcoming of evil there is great reward. George Eliot in *Romola* traces the patient struggle of the heroine against the perfidy of her false husband. In the epilogue, Romola speaks of a happiness she has gained in spite of her own private tragedy. She says: "We can only have the highest happiness . . . by having wide thoughts, and much feeling for the rest of the world as well as ourselves; and this sort of happiness often brings so much pain with it, that we can only tell it from pain by its being what we would choose before everything else, because our souls see it is good. There are so many things wrong and difficult in the world, that no man can be great . . . unless he gives up thinking about pleasure and rewards, and gets strength to endure what is hard and painful."

Assurance

St. Paul sketches the rungs in the ladder of confidence by which Christ's followers climb from the cave of suffering to the sunny heights of assurance. "We rejoice in our sufferings, knowing that suffering produces endurance, and endurance produces character, and character produces hope, and hope does not disappoint us, because God's love has been poured into our hearts through the Holy Spirit which has been given to us" (Rom. 5:3-5).

One of the things which has always strengthened my faith is this: that those who would seem to have the most reason to doubt the goodness of God are the firmest believers in his providence. Some years ago I knew a young woman whose deformed body was a house of torture. During her last illness, a young interne stopped beside her bed and said, "Why is it that you are so cheerful in all your pain while I who have every reason to be contented am so often grouchy?" The young woman looked up with a smile and said, "I have a secret." "What is it?" he asked. She replied, "God is love."

Curiously enough that confident affirmation comes from the poor and afflicted with more frequency than from the affluent and the healthy. It is those who have gone down into the depths of life who are most certain of its heights. It is the veterans of life with the most scars who believe the struggle is most worthwhile.

Professor Paul Tillich has made a study of the word "deep" as it is used in Scripture. The Bible speaks of the "deep things of God," meaning the deeper truths.

It also says, "Out of the depths have I cried unto thee," meaning thereby the deeper sufferings. The depth of suffering, says Tillich, "is the door, the only door, to the depth of truth!" Suffering endured with God leads to discovery of life's deeper truths. Pain can be a teacher and a purifier. God brings men into deep waters, not to drown them, but to cleanse them.[43]

This growing confidence which comes through pain can continue even to the gates of death. During the Korean conflict a letter came to my view written by Mrs. Soon Kim, the wife of Bishop Yu Soon Kim of Korea, to her son at Syracuse University. She tells of the bombings and brutality suffered. She and her husband stayed at their posts when the communists came to Seoul. The Bishop was investigated and harassed. Finally he was taken away. His friends believed he had been liquidated. But Mrs. Kim's letter showed no breaking of spirit, no dismal doubt, no loss of faith. She wrote: "I remembered the verse, 'We are his, alive or dead,' and rejoiced in the spirit of thankfulness."

How did she attain such undimmed assurance? Years ago she committed her will to Christ, the Way. Through her long service she has been dedicating her mind to seeking Christ the Truth. Through love and sacrifice she has lived her life into Christ the Life, and now, like the Great Apostle before her, she is "sure that neither death nor life, . . . nor things present nor things to come, . . . will be able to separate [her] from the love of God which is in Christ Jesus our Lord" (Rom. 8:38).

The assurance of God's care can carry with it a Christlike attitude toward those who cause the suffering. Mme. Chiang Kai-shek in *The Sure Victory* described her own ascent from the desire for vengeance to trust in God's justice and mercy. She wrote: "Determination and will power, however, are quite different from the power that comes from faith and prayer. About the third year of living half-underground . . . I came to a new point of spiritual desolation. I said my prayers and they meant nothing. They were just words. I realized that I was being slowly poisoned by resentment, hate and bitterness.

"Did you ever try to pray for an enemy? Have you ever tried to love someone who is ruining your life? . . . I could not ask blessings for the aggressors no matter how I tried. Surely even God could not demand that of me! . . ."

After visiting an orphanage of blind children she wrote: "Never had I realized so clearly . . . that the eyes are the windows of the soul. . . . I have always been repulsed by abnormality, whether mental or physical. . . . I asked myself whether I was not spiritually blind deliberately, when I hated. Then this thought flashed through my mind. If I am so repulsed by physical blindness and defacement how much more repulsed must God be by my spiritual blindness and ugliness? And our spiritual blindness is often willful and determined. . . . Then my ears seemed to echo my mother's voice saying: ' *"Vengeance is mine, saith the Lord."* It certainly isn't yours.' Thus I was enabled to unload my hate at the foot of the Cross. Now when I pray I can turn the enemy over to God, His mercy and His justice." [44]

We can catch the confidence of Katherine Stevenson in the lines:

> The gladdest messengers of all the past
>   Have worn disguise of sorrow or of pain:
> And can I doubt Thy love to me doth last
>   Or fear to trust Thy wisdom once again?
>   "My times are in Thy hand." [45]

Helpfulness

The late Dr. Ray Allen made a very suggestive translation of a familiar Beatitude: "Blessed are they that mourn for they shall be comforters." When we are going through deep waters, we turn for help to those who "have been through the mill."

"There is a church that carefully records the major experiences of its members," writes Oscar Blackwelder in *The Interpreter's Bible*. [A practice that is worth pondering!] "For example, a young couple lost their child; time and God helped to heal their grief. Another young couple several years later suffered the same loss. Beyond all other aid which the church could provide the first couple was able to help the second." [46]

The inspiration given by the example of a brave sufferer was realized by the brilliant Katherine Mansfield, who wrote near the end of her long and fatal illness: "I do not want to die without leaving a record of my belief that suffering can be overcome. For I do believe it. What must one do? There is no question of what is called 'passing beyond it.' This is false.

"One must submit. Take it. Be overwhelmed. Accept it fully. Make it part of life. Everything that we really accept undergoes a change. So suffering must become Love. . . . I must put my agony into something. Change it." [47]

Those who show an undefeated spirit in desperate circumstances do something for the race which success does not do. We are immeasurably helped by those who do not crack up when they might be expected to do so. Captain Scott did not reach the South Pole, but the courage he showed amid the Antarctic blizzard and the gallant way he carried on when all hope of escape was gone, did something more for the human race than any mere success of planting a flag at the South Pole.

A distinguished Southerner, Dr. Edwin Mims, said that Robert E. Lee did more for the South during the five years after Appomattox than during the five years he so brilliantly led his troops in the war. By maintaining an unbroken spirit free from bitterness, by demonstrating how defeat can be endured without recrimination and revenge, by carrying on in public service with the nobility of a Christian gentleman, Lee lifted the morale not only of the South but of the whole land.

A young man ran for the legislature in his state and was defeated. He entered business and failed because of a worthless partner. He fell passionately in love with a girl, but death took her from him. He was elected to Congress, served one term, and was defeated for reelection. He next tried to get an appointment to the United States Land Office and failed. He tried to be a lyceum lecturer, but was no success. He became a candidate for the United States Senate, and was defeated. He ran for the vice-presidency, and was defeated. And when at last he became President, he was at once engulfed in a war which he would have given his life to prevent, and, in fact, it was a war which did indirectly take his life. Can you think of any life in which so many defeats were telescoped together? And yet do we not feel that Abraham Lincoln is the most beloved and inspiring son America has produced?

As Emerson wrote of Lincoln: "He had a vast good nature, which made him tolerant and accessible to all; fair-minded, leaning to the claim of the petitioner; affable, and not sensible to the affliction which the innumerable visits paid to him when President would have brought to anyone else. And how this good nature became a noble humanity, in many a tragic case which the events of the war brought to him, everyone will remember; and with what increasing tenderness he dealt when a whole race was thrown on his compassion.

God has enabled men to use pain not only for their own enrichment but also for the strengthening of others. Yonder is a mother beside the bed of her feverish child. The little one keeps crying, "Mommy, mommy," as she tosses from side to side in her suffering. How the mother's heart breaks as she suffers with and for her child, but from that breaking mother-heart is somehow imparted to the child a strength and comfort which are not given by any cold, unfeeling care, however efficient and professional it may be.

Our manner of embracing a suffering child is symbolic and suggestive. We take it in our arms as if we would gather up its pain into our own body. So in our imagination we can think of our heavenly Father with his everlasting arms of mercy. He shares our sufferings as Christ suffered for us, leaving us an example that we should follow his steps.

A college student went to hear a speech by Kagawa, the great Japanese Christian who had more than once visited our shores. As he walked away from the meeting, he said to his minister who was with him: "I did not think Kagawa said anything very unusual. His remarks were rather obvious." He was silent awhile. Then he went on: "But I looked at the very thick lens of the glasses he wore and I remembered that Kagawa got that eye disease by working among the sufferers in the slums of Japan." He was again silent for a moment. Then he added: "I guess when a man is on a cross he doesn't have to say much."

No, the cross speaks for itself.

Turn now to a figure standing supreme above all others. St. Paul declared that the heart of his message was to "preach Christ crucified, a stumbling block to the Jews and folly to the Gentiles" (I Cor. 1:23). Paul could have presented Jesus Christ in a way that would have seemed acceptable both to the Greeks and the Jews. He could have cited the practical counsels which Jesus gave about handling one's body and mind. He could have cited sayings of Jesus which make for peace of mind and social acceptability and even financial success. And by picking out those pleasing words of Jesus, Paul could have drawn many to admire the Nazarene teacher who seemed so helpful, just as many can be drawn now to hear about Jesus, if we make him fit our modern patterns of success.

But the centuries have shown the wisdom of Paul's preaching Christ crucified rather than Christ the successful teacher. What holds the hearts of men to Christ through the ages is not that he taught the most beautiful principles, but that he was the teacher who died for his principles; not merely that he was the physician who healed with marvelous power, but that he was the physician who gave his own blood for his patients; not merely that he was the noble hero who showed how men can suffer, but that he was the Redeemer who revealed how God can suffer.

Truly "the Lord disciplines him whom he loves" and "for the moment all discipline is painful rather than pleasant" but "later it yields the peaceful fruit of righteousness to those who have been trained by it" (Heb. 12:11). Yea, "the sufferings of this present time are not worth comparing with the glory that is to be revealed to us" (Rom. 8:18).

CHAPTER V

Death

How to Face One's Own Death

The foundation of my belief in immortality reaches farther back than the resurrection of Christ. It rests on the very integrity of the universe. The belief in a life beyond the grave has persisted through all races. This conviction is strongest in our healthiest moments and rises out of our noblest emotion, that of love. The Creator has endowed us with the power to love, to evaluate, to hope. These powers are as integral to human nature as the craving of the body for food and drink and air. Surely the Creator who keeps faith with the appetites of our bodies will not play false with the hungers of our souls.

If life ended at the grave, this would seem an irrational world. It would mean that the universe, having groaned in travail to bring forth its highest creation, human personality, then tosses it into the dust heap, a piece of rotting flesh less valuable than rusting iron which can be salvaged for future use. In this universe we are told there is conservation of energy, and the light of a candle does not stop when the flame is extinguished but goes on traveling through space. Can we then believe that the light of love which shone in the eyes of our dead dear ones has vanished into nothingness? No. In a universe whose physical laws we can so trust that we build skyscrapers seventy stories high, surely we can trust the highest longings of our spirits.

When we behold, with Bryant, the Power whose care teaches the way of the waterfowl along the pathless coast, "lone wandering, but not lost," we go on to say with him:

> He who, from zone to zone,
> Guides through the boundless sky thy certain flight,
> In the long way that I must tread alone,
> Will lead my steps aright.[49]

And Christ by his life's teaching has enhanced our belief in the fidelity of the Creator. He taught that the ruler of this world is a heavenly Father, who clothes the grass of the fields and feeds the fowls of the air, who is more eager than earthly fathers to give good things to his children. And Christ so lived what he taught that men beheld in his face the glory of God. Since water does not rise higher than its source, the Christ who became flesh must have come from a heavenly Father as good as he was. And if God be as good as Christ, I for one feel that I can trust him both for this world and whatever may come after.

Moreover, the work of Christ did not end on Calvary. When I let my mind lie open to the record, and allow each Gospel to bring its wave of testimony in on my thought, I feel a rising tide of conviction that Christ did triumph over the grave.

The sorrowful women going out in the misty morning to anoint the body of their departed Leader; the experience at the tomb which sent them rushing back to bring the disciples; the evening walk to Emmaus when a mysterious presence seemed to accompany them and to make their hearts burn within them on the way; the upper room a week later with the disciples gathered around the still doubting Thomas, and then his cry of conviction, "My Lord, and my God"—these were the Easter reports, and they were told with such restraint and artlessness that I cannot believe they were inventions. Nor can I think of them as ghost stories told by deluded, though perhaps honest, persons. What ghost ever had the effect of producing moral grandeur in the people who thought they saw him? Yet that is what the Resurrection did for the disciples. It transformed them from defeated refugees into triumphant radiant apostles proclaiming their risen Lord.

Why then do we have such fear of death that we are ever fleeing from it and casting frightened glances over our shoulder at this stern spectre which dogs our steps? Perhaps this failure to look death in the face is partly the cause of our fear. It does seem that those who have come closest to death in battle or in serious illness develop a kind of calm courage. Among the treasured bits of literature are some letters left by Dr. Edward Wilson, the brave and brilliant explorer who lost his life in the Antarctic. Listen to his words written to his wife as he knew the end was near: "Don't be unhappy. We are playing a good part in a great scheme arranged by God himself, and all is well. . . . We will all meet after death and death hath no terrors . . . all is for the best to those who have loved God, and we have both loved him with all our lives."

Such courage has the Christlike quality, for it was in that spirit that Christ walked toward the cross. He knew he was about to die. For one half hour in Gethsemane he prayed that the cross might be avoided; but he arose saying, "Not my will but thine be done." Having surrendered his will, he took his death in his stride, saying to his comrades: "Let not your heart be troubled, neither let it be afraid" (John 14:27, K.J.V.).

When we look death in the face with the consciousness of our heavenly Father's love, the grave loses most of its dread. Is it the pain of dying that we fear?

Physicians assure us that quite usually the actual pain at the time of passing is less than many of the pains we endure in living. And when we catch the spirit of the Great Physician, the physical aspects of dying lose their terrors. One of the most saintly souls in my circle of acquaintances was Bishop Berggrav, the primate of Norway. You will remember him as the heroic figure who resisted the Nazi invasion of Norway and was placed under house arrest, where he lived for months in the shadow of possible death. When he was asked about his view of death, he answered with a simple story. One day a peasant took his little son on a visit to a village some distance away. On the road, they had to cross a swift stream which was spanned by a rickety narrow bridge. It was dark when they started home. The boy remembered the shaky bridge and was frightened. His father, noticing his fears, lifted the lad up and carried him in his arms. In a few minutes the little fellow was fast asleep on his father's shoulder. When he awoke, he was at home with the morning sun streaming through the window of his bedroom. Such was Bishop Berggrav's description of the act of dying.

What is it we dread about death? Perhaps it is the loss of what we have loved here on earth—our homes, our possessions, our loved ones. And here too, Christ helps us, if we let him. During our days here Christ would set us to living with lasting things. He would turn our gaze and thoughts from "the things that are seen and temporal" to "the things that are invisible and eternal." He told us to transfer our hearts' affections to the treasures which "neither moth nor rust consumes and where thieves do not break through and steal" (Matt. 6:20).

If we learn to value character and love more than

lands and cars, then we are getting our treasures into the form we can take with us.

Or does our dread of death stem from the thought of being cheated? The Grim Reaper cuts us off before we have had a chance to finish our work. Or perhaps, as Dr. Michalson has said, "the thought of death makes us feel that any effort we make will be wasted in work that will never reach fruition and hence will be futile." He cites the case of a young German soldier facing almost certain death in the battle for Stalingrad and quotes his last letter in which he wrote: "I have no fear, but my heart is sad. . . . A hollow indifference has seized me and cripples every activity. . . . It does not pay to fight and die for this shadow world." [50]

In contrast to this mood is the Christian conviction that Jesus did not prepare for death as a man getting ready for retirement but rather as one preparing for a larger work. He seemed to consider death as just a step through a door to another room in his Father's house. He shed no tears of farewell. He left the earth not as if the light of day were behind him. He faced death saying gallantly, "Be of good cheer, I have overcome the world" (John 16:33).

When we see how Jesus lived and loved and died; when we behold his face free from any shadow of fear as he approached the cross; when we see how he entered the grave, as well as how he triumphed over it; we understand the mood of Victor Hugo when he said: "I have come, as other men say, to the end of the day. But I cannot say to the end of my work, for the tomb is not a blind alley. It is a passing from light through darkness to dawn."

May it be that we suffer from the fear of judgment after death? Let us not make light of divine judgment. "The sting of death is sin" (I Cor. 15:56). But let us not torture ourselves with the medieval pictures of fiery torment. Jesus revealed God as a Father and a father punishes in order to redeem. But endless, hopeless hell cannot be reconciled with Christ's concept of a loving heavenly Father. As Carl Michalson says, we have "a reliable clue" to God's judgment in the incarnation, passion, and death of Christ. "For God has already judged the world in Christ, and he has said yes. He has stated His purpose is reconciliation and not condemnation. He has shown himself to be a God of mercy. 'For our sake he made him to be sin who knew no sin, so that we might become the righteousness of God' (II Cor. 5:21). This knowledge is enough to pull the sting of death and liberate us from the second death of guilt." [51]

The more I study the Gospels, the more I come to believe that we pass from this life to the next by way of a schoolroom rather than by way of a courtroom. Eternal life is the extension of the courses we take here. God gives us another chance but he does not change the rules of the school. God is just to reward us, even "exceeding abundantly above all that we ask or think," but the rewards are in line with what we have earned. We go on from where we are in the course. If we have not learned much of good in this life, we shall have to start the next life without much of good. But if we have learned to follow Christ, the Way, and to seek Christ, the Truth, we shall be ready to live with Christ, the Life.

Still another consideration shadows many minds as they think about death. Death seems to take us from objects that make life worth living—our homes, our loved ones, our prized possessions, our activities and associations. Will not life be empty and unreal without these?

How can we make the future life seem alive and real? Let me use a very inadequate analogy. Suppose a Californian became stranded among the Eskimos in some snowbound region of Alaska. How would he make Southern California real to the Eskimos? I am using Southern California as my analogy of heaven because those who live there think it is the nearest thing to heaven which earth affords! Well, the man from Southern California would have to describe his home to the Eskimos mostly in negatives, would he not, because they could hardly comprehend palm trees and oranges. So he would say to them there is no ice there, no whale-meat there, no midnight sun.

Similarly the Scripture describes heaven mostly in negatives. "There shall be no night there" (Rev. 33:5), no weeping, no wailing. Since spiritual things have to be spiritually discerned, we have no adequate way of describing heaven in our material terms. The Bible can only say that "this perishable nature must put on the imperishable, and this mortal nature must put on immortality" (I Cor. 15:53), that "if the earthly tent we live in is destroyed, we have a building from God, a house not made with hands, eternal in the heavens" (II Cor. 5:1). All this is rather hard to make real and living, isn't it?

But Jesus so lived and taught that he brought glimpses of the kingdom of heaven into the here and now. He said, "The kingdom of God is in the midst of you" (Luke 17:21). We too have experiences in which we forget time, when the pulse beats faster, and as Scott says, "one crowded hour of glorious life is worth an age without a name." And we exclaim, "Ah, this is heavenly." And we do have those moments of rare insight and lofty feeling when, as the Scripture says, we have "tasted the powers of the age to come" (Heb. 6:5).

Christ makes foretastes of the future available to us if we learn to like what he liked, if we look on the things that are invisible and eternal until they become real to us. It is by giving attention to things that we make them real to us. In my boyhood community when a young man was making love to a girl, the neighbors said that he was "paying attention to her." True, that is the way we make love. And if we would make eternal life real and appealing to ourselves, we must give attention to whatsoever things are true, and honest, and just, and pure, and lovely; we must set our values on the inner qualities of life, on character rather than reputation, on being something rather than having something. When we do this, we are, as Jesus said, laying up treasures in heaven "where thieves do not break in and steal" (Matt. 6:20). Remember this, if you live for what you *have,* you can't take it with you. But if you live for what you *are* in mind and heart, you have something moth and rust cannot corrupt and death cannot destroy.

One of the most helpful ways of thinking about the hereafter was expressed in the story of a doctor who was calling on a patient in his terminal illness. The patient said that he believed in a future life but "asked the doctor if he had any conviction as to what awaited him in the life beyond." The doctor was momentarily at a loss, but just then he heard a scratching at the door. It was his dog which had followed him on his round of calls. "Do you hear that?" he asked his patient. "That is my dog. I left him downstairs, but he grew impatient and has come up and hears my voice. He has no notion what is inside that door, but he knows I am here. Now is it not the same with you? You do not know what lies beyond the Door, but you know your Master is there." [52]

We do not know the details of the future abode, but the Christian does trust our Lord's promise, "I go to prepare a place for you" (John 14:2).

> I know not where His islands lift
>   Their fronded palms in air;
> I only know I cannot drift
>   Beyond His love and care.[53]

A few years ago a friend passed away. He was a scholar, Doctor of Philosophy from Columbia University; he was a distinguished missionary, doctor of souls in China for forty years. The guiding prayer of his life was: "O God, our Father, I accept thy gift of love; help me to pass it on for Jesus' sake." On the morning of his death at 92, Dr. Lacey Sites said to those at his bedside: "If we live the eternal life now, we will always."

Such is the confidence Christ's love has kindled in his devoted followers from St. Paul to the present. Surely God will keep faith with those who love him most. "Love never ends."

How to Accept the Death of a Loved One

Memory can come to our aid in our sorrow. The thoughts of previous separations can serve as stairs in the climb toward comfort.

Have we not all, as Douglas Steere suggests, outlived some "little deaths"?

Recall the day when as a parent we saw our child off to his first day at school. We saw him launch out to be on his own little self. We imagined the things that might happen to him with us not there to watch over him. We died a little death that morning when he disappeared from our sight. But out of that experience "he became more our own, because we let him go."

Recall the day we gave a daughter in marriage. "How

great the risks and uncertainties of love and marriage!" Would that young man know how to take care of our precious girl? We died another little death when we gave her away, but out of that came an enlarged love embracing two instead of one.[54]

Recall the day when we said good-bye to a son or daughter on the way to war. The dangers ahead, the uncertainty of return, the aching loneliness made that departure another death. But we outlived it, for distance did not break the tie that binds.

And some of us can recall when we laid a loved one away. He was part of us, flesh of our flesh, and when he left he fairly tore the heart out of us. But years pass and he is still with us. We can hear the tones of his voice. We can see his little beloved mannerisms. He still lives in our hearts. Thus we outlived another death.

We can show our fortitude by meeting our sorrow with dignity. Much is written about the professionalizing and paganizing of our funeral services. But personally I have been deeply impressed by the way in which funeral services bring out the nobler qualities of the mourners. Especially is this observable among those in the humble walks of life. The sympathy manifested by friends and the silent gratitude of the bereaved for the comradeship of those who have come to pay their respects demonstrate the truth of the hymn,

> Blest be the tie that binds
> Our hearts in Christian love;
> The fellowship of kindred minds
> Is like to that above.[55]

To be sure, funeral services are sometimes conducted in a manner that is harrowing, but to abolish them would be hardening. The sharing of sorrow in a dignified service of remembrance brings out the "better angels of our natures."

Also, as we listen to the scriptural promises read at the services, our faith is strengthened. Some years ago a young woman, after her father's funeral service, expressed her faith thus: "Every time the door swings to let a loved one through from the world of the visible to the world of the invisible, I feel more confidence in the divine care."

Grief tends to leave our minds numb. But we should try to meet the loss of loved ones with understanding. St. Augustine, after the death of his best friend and his mother, asserted that people undergo acute grief generally for two reasons. One, they love others as if they would never die. We should school ourselves for loss by loving others as mortals. Also, they look upon death as a loss and mourn for their losses, because they hold to the lives of others as if they possessed those lives. They should remember that only God really possesses the lives of others.

Philip of Macedon gave to his slave a standing order. Every morning he was to enter the royal quarters and shout, "Philip, remember that thou must die." [56] It would be well if we substituted for "thou" the word "they," and remembered daily that those we love most dearly are mortal, even as we are.

The Greek stoics taught that a man should not love his wife or child too much and then he would not be devastated by their death. But this virtue of emotionlessness, "apathia," is rather cold comfort in contrast to the Christian attitude of loving to the utmost, assured that (life is too great for the grave and love can never lose its own.)

Some years ago during Holy Week, Dean Inge of St. Paul's Cathedral, London, lost his eleven-year-old daughter. Out of his grief, Dean Inge, whose mind was rated the most brilliant in England at the time, wrote:

"If we are right in claiming for our judgments of value an authority no less than we allow to our judgments of fact, which come to us through the senses, we may assert with confidence that the souls of the righteous are in the hand of God, and that what is dear to Him will never be plucked out of the land of the living." [57]

Instead of dwelling on the loss we have suffered in the death of our loved ones, we can think gratefully of the gift we have received from God in sharing their lives. Some years ago a young man died at twenty-one just after he had finished a long and expensive education. The bereaved parents will never forget the words spoken to them at the time by the late Dr. Walter A. Jessup, former president of the State University of Iowa. Dr. Jessup told of a father who had lost two sons just as they were about to launch forth on their lifework. The father said that his boys had given him far more satisfaction than could be measured by any money and efforts spent on them and hence he still felt indebted to God for their lives.

In similar vein William Allen White wrote at the death of his daughter, killed at the age of 17: "Mrs. White and I are standing on our feet, realizing that the loss is heavy and the blow is hard, but not beating our hands against the bars and asking why. On our books Mary is a net gain. She was worth so much more than she cost, and she left so much more behind than she took away that we are flooded with joyous memories and cannot question either the goodness of God or the general decency of man." [58]

Another anodyne for grief is work. As Betsey Barton watched her mother being drawn toward death in the coils of cancer, she fortified her own spirit by continued activity, realizing that "One must go on living even while there is dying to do." [59]

Longfellow's poetic genius may be questioned by many, but he had about him what Van Wyck Brooks calls a "moral magic." And nowhere was this better shown than in the way Longfellow continued his work after the death of his wife, throwing himself into his translation of Dante with a spirit which radiated cheer to his coterie of co-workers. To transmute suffering into service is great living.

(Beyond all other sources of comfort in the hour of sorrow is the Christian hope of reunion after death)

Thomas Jefferson's religious beliefs would not be considered thoroughly orthodox, but he was sustained by conviction of God's eternal care. When he was dying, he told his daughter Martha that he had left in a drawer something for her to read when he was gone. This is what he had written: "On that shore which shall crown all my hopes, or drown all my cares, I hope to meet two seraphs, long vanished, my beloved wife and my daughter Maria."

Emerson attained the same assurance by the hard road of reason. After the death of his son, he wrote:

> *What is excellent*
> *As God lives, is permanent;*
> *Hearts are dust, hearts' loves remain;*
> *Hearts' love will meet thee again.*
> Death cannot hold my beautiful boy.[60]

It is related of Oliver Cromwell that "a few days after [his daughter's death], confined to his room, he asked for his Bible and read the passage, 'I have learned in whatsoever state I am therewith to be content. . . . I can do all things, through Christ which strengtheneth me.' Turning to Harvey [his friend] he said, 'This Scripture did once save my life, when my eldest son

(Robert) died, which went as a dagger to my heart, indeed it did.' Paul had learned that lesson, and as he revolved the words his [Cromwell's] faith rose triumphant, 'He that was Paul's Christ is my Christ too,' he said."

Later, as his own death neared, Cromwell said, " 'The Lord hath filled me with as much assurance of His pardon and His love as my soul can hold. . . . I am a conqueror, more than a conqueror, through Christ that strengtheneth me.' " And toward the end, "Harvey heard him frequently say with much cheerfulness, and fervor of spirit, 'God is good.' " [61]

Since God is love and Christ craved comradeship, we can believe that there will be fellowship in the hereafter. I believe that we shall know our loved ones better in the spirit realm than here where we see through a glass darkly, and alas, where we often are too hurried to look at them. And I believe that we shall have fellowship with many who in this world are fenced off by class and color and creed, for I agree with Frederick William Faber when he sang:

> For the love of God is broader
>   Than the measure of man's **mind**,
> And the heart of the Eternal
>   Is most wonderfully kind.[62]

Up at Dartmouth College there is a building known as Dick Hall's house, erected in memory of a lad who died in 1917. In the house is a book with a famous inscription written by another father who had lost a boy. That other father was Calvin Coolidge. And here are the words he wrote in the house book: "To Edward K. Hall: In recollection of his son and my son, who have the privilege by the grace of God to be boys through all eternity."

That inscription, of course, raises a question: Will the loved ones we knew here as boys and babies still be boys and babies yonder? We cannot presume to say. We are content with the scriptural assurance given centuries ago: "Beloved, we are God's children now: it does not yet appear what we shall be, but we know that when he appears we shall be like him, for we shall see him as he is" (I John 3:2).

And the assurance of future reunion is deepened by present cultivation of communion with our departed loved ones. Some Christians pray for the dead. Others condemn the practice because they think it presumptuous to assume that our prayers will alter God's treatment of the dead. We rightly reject the idea that living persons, by any payments to a church, can produce better treatment for their loved ones beyond the veil. Nevertheless, if we can commune in spirit with persons in other parts of this earth, it would seem reasonable that we can commune with the souls living beyond its limits. And such communion can be sanely cultivated by thought and prayer.

Sir William Ramsay, the eminent scholar, once talked to a friend of mine, Dr. William P. King, about the son he had lost in World War I. Sir William said: "The communion with that son is a spiritual communion. That son is with me more than all the other children. He does me more good than the others for I feel that I must be always ready to meet him."

Yes, for the sake of that son we lost or that mother who is waiting, for the sake of the things they did for us and the things we forgot or failed to do for them, for the sake of these, we consecrate ourselves. And our faith is that our lives are still linked with theirs through God. "Wherefore seeing we also are compassed about with so great a cloud of witnesses"—those who have gone before—"let us lay aside every weight, and the sin that doth so easily beset us, . . . looking unto Jesus the author and finisher of our faith" (Heb. 12:1-2, K.J.V.).

How to Help Those Who Are Bereaved

John Morley, the English statesman and man of letters, in an address made in Edinburgh in 1887, said: "The great business of life is to be, to do, to do without, and to depart." Take those succinct phrases. "To be"—the full rich personalities God planned us to be and our mothers dreamed we would be. "To do"—the things we are capable of doing, and leaving the world better for our labors. "To do without"—to be able to lose things without losing heart, to make the most of what we have left. "And to depart"—leaving the stage of life with grace and dignity, unashamed and unafraid, having learned what we can't take with us and what we can.

Yes, as John Morley said, the great business of life is "to be, to do, to do without, and to depart." And if we are to make it great, we must learn to know the things that last.

Professor Walter Horton of Oberlin tells that a girl in one of his classes wrote in her paper that she did not feel the need of believing in God because she was engaged to be married, and her whole life revolved quite adequately around the man she loved. Professor Horton said he trembled for her because he knew the man, and while he was a nice enough fellow, he lacked several important qualifications for the role of deity.

No living human being is an adequate object of worship, as a substitute for God, if for no other reason than that of impermanence. Shakespeare shows how Cardinal Wolsey revealed his discovery of that fact:

> Had I but served my God with half the zeal

> I served my king, he would not in mine age
> Have left me naked to mine enemies.⁶³

(When we get completely wrapped up in some human object of love, we are almost sure eventually to be left naked by death or disillusionment.)

Our human loves are safeguarded only when they are gathered up into the divine love. We must learn to love the lasting elements in our human affections. (The marriage bond becomes permanent only as it develops mental and spiritual ties.) Mere physical attraction is likely to wane unless there is a weaving together of hearts and minds by common interests and shared sacrifices. Love between parent and child must have more than a physical basis if it is to last and grow. Parents cannot expect children to show them proper affection just because they gave them birth and a home in infancy. There must be cultivation of spiritual bonds through companionship, confidence, and cooperation.

And if we are to learn to love the lasting elements in our relationships and our enviroment, we must train our taste. Good tastes, you know, do not come easily. We can pick up cheap tastes, cheap tunes, cheap humor, on the street or almost anywhere. But to acquire a taste for the masterpieces of art, for the best music, for the things that last—all this requires time and much living with.

One summer I was shown through Chartres Cathedral which contains probably the most exquisite stained glass in the world. The frail little man who guided us was said to be France's greatest expert on ecclesiastical glass. I watched his radiant face as he explained the beauty and significance of the windows. A year later in Paris I learned that he had passed away. But somehow I could not feel that he had passed from life. He had looked so long on what St. Paul called the "things that are invisible and eternal," that he had come to love them and live with them. And who shall separate us from the love of divine and eternal things? "Shall tribulation, or distress, or persecution, or famine, or nakedness, or peril, or sword?" "No!" shouts the Great Apostle, "in all these things we are more than conquerors through him who loved us" (Rom. 8:37).

The Art of Leaving

We suffer the loss not only of things that are taken from us but also of experiences and situations which we have to leave. Have we learned how to leave? Have we learned how to move from one locality in order to make our homes in some new community? Have we learned how to pass from a great thrill or a deep sorrow without suffering a paralyzing aftereffect? The art of leaving is a very vital part of the art of living.

I think of a bit of inspired counsel given by the prophet Isaiah to a people whom he was calling to leave the city of Babylon. I should like to place it before you as a formula for the art of leaving. This is the advice, which Isaiah gives to his people of Israel on leaving Babylon: "You shall not go in haste," or as Moffatt's translation puts it, "Nor need you hurry forth, flying like fugitives, for the Lord will go before you, and the God of Israel will be your rear guard" (Isa. 52:12).

Have we learned how to leave our pleasant experiences? (Does the memory of the loved places we have left go with us as inspiration to enrich our future days or does it leave us with a nostalgia that spoils the good times ahead?) Jesus did not rush through his days as if impatient to go on to the next task. He took time to play with little children, to mingle with wedding guests, to enter into the domestic joys of home circles. On the other hand, he cautioned his followers against looking back with futile regret to the little things left behind. ('No one who puts his hand to the plow and looks back is fit for the kingdom of God") (Luke 9:62).

Our Lord would have his followers enter fully into the experience of the moment unclouded by regret and unhurried by impatience. The grammar of growth involves the proper use of all three tenses—past, present, and future. Through memory we should preserve the past in such a way that it enriches the present and prepares us for the future.

Let us not succumb to the mood of restlessness, rushing from place to place and from thrill to thrill, so impatient for the latest thing that we miss the lasting thing. On the other hand, as Jesus said, let us "remember Lot's wife" and not look back to what we are leaving when we should be looking ahead.

Also, have we learned how to leave our sad experiences? Some seek escape from sad memories by a change of scene. To get away from the environmental reminders of our sorrow may pluck some of the nettles from our wounded spirits. A minister once told me that after the death of his wife he took a trip to another city and went to a ball game. He said that he simply had to have a change of scene to relieve his sorrow. His grief, I believe, was sincere, but to seek the cure of sorrow in mere diversion seems almost irreverent. I have known anguished hearts, however, that found healing from the ravages of death by visiting the lovely gardens of old Charleston, or by going to the seashore where the illimitable ocean with its unceasing ebb and flow symbolizes the eternal.

Some try to get away from their sorrows by throwing themselves into their work. Viscount Grey, writing toward the close of World War I, said that the best thing for anyone who had to bear great sorrow was work. Those who had work to do and the strength to do it and who could sleep, he said, would be able to endure life day by day. Since man does not "live in a lump" but only day by day, each day would bring its quota of work and "some expedient" to help one endure the pain of living.

Yes, work may be an opiate for grief, but remember it remains an anodyne rather than a remedy. The mind is distracted but the ache in the heart is not cured. Furthermore, do we want to solace our grief by mere forgetting? Ah, no, that one we loved and lost we do not want to put out of mind. We want to hold him in the shrine of our memory. And that is what God helps us to do when he goes along with us in our sorrows. God keeps green the memory of our beloved dead so that we think of them, not as lying lonely in some snowcovered mound, but living in another room of our Father's house of many mansions. When a boy brings his troubles to a father, these troubles enable the boy to get closer to the father's heart and help the father to enter further into the boy's confidence. So sorrow rightly shared with God gives a new quality to our faith, a new depth to our understanding, a new power to our prayers, a new lift to our sympathy.

But how does God protect us from the pursuing past? Does God "pluck from the memory a rooted sorrow" or "raze out the written troubles of the brain?" When we think how our world is so bedeviled by festering memories, old wounds, embedded prejudices, smoldering hatreds, we almost feel that it would be well for God to strike humanity with a complete loss of memory and allow us to start a new world wherein old scores and sorrows are forgotten.

God does not wipe out the memory of the evils we

have suffered or the sins we have committed. The scars remain. But he floods those memories with his forgiving grace. He can transform our very wounds into sources of strength.

> He breaks the power of cancelled sin;
> He sets the prisoner free.

God leaves us with our past, but takes away its control over us. That wrong we did we can still remember, but with God's help we do not repeat it. That old prejudice which we cherished may still linger in memory to shame us, but it no longer has power over us. The remembrance of our sins humbles us, but the sins themselves can no longer humiliate us. That is what God does. Remorse is changed to repentance when "the God of Israel [is our] rear guard."

In life we must learn the art of leaving—leaving our homes and our loved ones, leaving our joys and our sorrows. But remember, God goes along. The Eternal goes in front of us, and our rear guard is Israel's God. With this guarding presence we can face any future, even death itself.

CHAPTER VI

The Fellowship of Suffering

Must the Good Pay for the Bad?

Now and then we read of some man who has been in prison for quite a period and then another person turns up and makes a confession, thereby clearing the prisoner of guilt. I have tried to think how it would be if I were in prison, scorned by the people that knew me, maligned and deserted for something I did not do. Certainly it would turn the mind to bitterness of thought.

Think how many people do suffer for things done by others. Numbers of people are killed who are termed "good drivers," but they are struck down on the roads by the recklessness of others. Little children are born into the world with blinded eyes and deformed bodies because, as the Bible says, "the iniquity of the fathers [is visited] upon the children, . . . to the third and the fourth generation" (Ex. 34:7).

Families in Korea were driven back and forth across that country, starved and left to die, because armies were seething over Korea seeking political sovereignty. And scientists tell us that generations beyond measure may be born weakened in bone and blood because governments persist in poisoning the air with nuclear testings.

These facts we face. What do we say about them? We can understand why people would be punished as retribution for guilt. We can understand, too, why some of our punishment and suffering is disciplinary, but to be caught in the web of circumstance and suffer for what others do, that is hard to understand.

Now of course when we stop to see just how far we are completely innocent, we find it difficult to draw a clear line. Suppose a boy goes bad and brings shame on his family. The parents will search their minds in anguish to know whether they failed at some point. And only God knows those subtle influences in the meshwork of family life which are responsible for misconduct.

Or suppose war did break out, and some night bombs were dropped on New York, reducing the city to a rubble like Hiroshima. If we survived and crawled up out of the ruins, could we be quite sure that we had no part in the blame for that war? Did we exercise all our efforts when we had the time to prevent war? Did we do our best to break through the curtains and spread good will?

We are so caught in a net of human relationships it is hard to draw the line between innocence and guilt.

Perhaps the best figure to describe this situation was given, back in the first book of Samuel, by Abigail—Nabal's wife. David and his troops were trying to clear the enemies out of Israel and they wanted food and supplies from their supporters. There was a farmer named Nabal living in the Carmel region. He was rich but he was churlish and suspicious. David sent some of his young men to ask for food and Nabal said: "Who is David? Who is the son of Jesse? Shall I take my bread and my water and my meat . . . and give it to men who come from I do not know where?" (I Sam. 25:10-11). When David learned of it he was angry and said, "Surely in vain have I guarded all that this fellow has in the wilderness . . . and he has returned me evil for good. God do so to David and more also, if by morning I leave so much as one male of all who belong to him" (21-22). Then Abigail, Nabal's wife, beautiful and generous [as she is pictured], prepared food, meat, wine, bread, and went forth to meet David. She made obeisance to him and said: "Upon me alone, my lord, be the guilt" (I Sam. 25:23). She went on to say that she did not know when the young men came, but that now she had brought food that they might take and spare Nabal. And then she said these words: "The life of my lord [i.e. David] shall be bound in the bundle of the living in the care of the LORD your God" (I Sam. 25:10-11, 21-29). We are "bound in the bundle of living." No man liveth or dieth to himself. We are bound together by the words we say, by the very thoughts which color the looks of our eyes and by the attitudes of our gestures, by the contagion of our vices and our diseases, by the consequences of our virtues and our conduct.

And the bad cannot completely pay for their badness. We cannot pay for a sin fully. Suppose I uttered some malicious word of gossip yesterday. That word is out in the atmosphere of the community and I can no more call back its effects than I can recapture the breath that left my nostrils yesterday.

Suppose I injected into some group an unwholesome influence last week? I can no more pull that out today than I can extract the ink that I pour into a pitcher of water. Ink and water flow together. So do sins. Because we cannot pay for our sins fully, because they are woven together like this in the bundle of life, we face the fact that the good do pay very often for the bad.

Indeed, the taxes we pay to the government are in part a burden which the strong carry for the lawless.

The insurance on our cars is increased by the reckless drivers around us.

Yet, making full allowance for all this that we have to pay for, think of the assets of our incorporated America. Think what people have done for us. Think of this "land of the pilgrims' pride." Think of the protection that our general stability of government gives us. Think of the opportunities we have in this comparatively free country. And I ask you: "Is there any person who does not feel he is getting more from America than he can pay for?"

"At Williams College when Mark Hopkins was president, some damage was done to a building. They found the culprit, who was the son of a wealthy man. The young fellow was hauled before the president. He pulled out his pocketbook and said, 'Well, doctor, how much is the damage?' Mark Hopkins said. 'Young man, put up your pocketbook. Tomorrow at prayers you will make public acknowledgment of your offense, or you will be expelled.' Hopkins later went on to tell how professors were sacrificing to give them an education, how men had sacrificed to found the college. 'Every man here is a charity student,' he said." [64] Whatever the tuition we pay in a college today, we do not pay the full cost. Whatever taxes we pay today, we are not paying the full price of what we get from America, because in the corporation of our country we do some things together which we cannot do by ourselves.

Turn now to the family. Who can balance the books of a family? That mother in her sleepless nights, getting up to care for the child that cries, that father spending long hours after others have gone to bed trying to figure out how to make both ends meet. Who can pay fully for that?

Suppose the Lord's Prayer went like this: "Our

Father, who art in heaven, hallowed be Thy name. Thy kingdom come, Thy will be done on earth as it is in heaven. Give us this day our daily bread and help us to collect the debts we paid for others yesterday." Would not that spoil the prayer completely? Ah, what that prayer leaves in the mind of the petitioner is that when we contemplate God in his heaven and the giving of the daily bread in the past, we are in debt: "Forgive us our debts as we forgive our debtors."

Every good person feels that though he has had to pay for the badness of others, he still has not paid his full way.

In the First Epistle of Peter are these words: "It is better to suffer for doing right, if that should be God's will, than for doing wrong. For Christ also died for sins once for all, the righteous for the unrighteous, that he might bring us to God" (I Peter 3:17-18).

Here we see that the paying of the good for the bad is a part of God's plan of salvation.

If we go back far enough into primitive times, we find that people thought God demanded the best human beings as human sacrifices. Men had to take the best they had and pay them to the gods as the price of appeasement.

Even the Greeks, whom we admire for their brilliance of mind, had in their mythology the story of Agamemnon and Iphigenia. The Greek fleet was on its way to Troy to avenge the abduction of Helen. It was becalmed in the harbor of Aulis. Agamemnon, the leader, took that occasion to go hunting and he killed a stag. But the stag was supposed to be under the special protection of the Greek goddess, Diana. Whereupon in vengeance upon Agamemnon she sent a pestilence on the becalmed fleet. Then they called in Calchas, the soothsayer, who said that the only thing that could appease

Diana would be to offer the best they had: some pure, noble maid. So they picked out Iphigenia, the daughter of Agamemnon. She was about to be married. To add to the horror the soothsayer said that her father, Agamemnon, must do the killing. They took her out to kill her, but she was rescued just at the point of death by Diana, who appeared and put a hind in place of the maiden and took her off to be a priestess in the temple at Tauris.

This concept of human sacrifice almost got into Hebrew practice. We see it in the story of Abraham and Isaac. Word came to Abraham, as he thought, that God wanted him to take his son Isaac up and slay him on an altar in the mountains. Just as he was about to drive the knife into the lad, he heard a voice saying that he had proven his faith. Therefore he could spare his son. And Abraham saw a ram, and he put the ram in place of Isaac (Gen. 22:1-13).

The Bible, however, shows how the Hebrew people rose from the primitive concept that required the innocent Isaac as a sacrificial victim for the sin of the people to the concept of One, our Lord Christ, who went willingly to sacrifice, not to placate an angry God, but to prove the love of God. That is what Peter meant when he said: "For Christ died for our sins, . . . the righteous for the unrighteous, that he might bring us to God."

Get the contrast: Isaac, taken by force to pay for man's badness; Jesus going willingly to prove God's goodness. He said, "No man taketh it [my life] from me; but I lay it down of myself" (John 10:18, K.J.V.). He went with the joy that was set before him. He endured the shame because that is God's way of bringing his children to him.

LIFE'S DEEPEST LAW

Firmly embedded in the mind of the race is the maxim, "Self-preservation is nature's first law." Wherever we look we see life struggling to preserve itself. The little "flower in the crannied wall," which Tennyson said would explain the universe if one could understand it, that little flower is sinking its roots and lifting its petals in a brave effort to save itself. Consider the fowls of the air. They build their nests, shelter their young and migrate with the seasons, all as a part of the instinct for self-preservation. Look through the miscroscope at your own blood stream. If a blood vessel is wounded, an army of white corpuscles is rushed to the defense, all as a part of this same principle of self-preservation. The cry of the wolf in the pack, the concern for health which sends us to a doctor, the building of air raid shelters, the struggle of a boy to equip himself with knowledge or a trade, the raising of armies, the conference of diplomats around a peace table—do not all these stem from the main root of man's desire for self-preservation? And is not this desire the first law of nature? Well, that is the belief on which we have been reared.

In the light of this law of self-preservation, how are we to explain the self-sacrifice which Jesus taught and supremely demonstrated when he deliberately laid down his life on the cross? Or to come nearer home, how do we account for the acts of heroic sacrifice which take place around us in our time—the mother giving her life for her child, the fireman dying to rescue the occupant of a burning building, the soldier risking death for his country?

We recall what they said to Jesus. When they beheld him hanging on the cross, some cried sarcastically: "He saved others; himself he cannot save. If he be the King of Israel, let him now come down from the cross, and we will believe him" (Matt. 27:42, K.J.V.). However cruel those words were, they sounded pretty plausible. There on the cross was a man who had gone about professing to save people. He allowed man to call him Lord. He presumed to speak in the name of God as master of life and death. Surely if he really possessed such power, he would use it to save himself.

How are we to explain Jesus' principle of self-sacrifice which was climaxed by the cross? Was Jesus trying to repeal the natural law of self-preservation? We believe not. Jesus was a realist. He knew what was in man. The Great Physician was well aware of life's basic drives and desires. He saw man's craving for health, and he was a healer. He understood how men longed for life, liberty, and the pursuit of happiness, and he said: "I am come that they might have life and have it abundantly" (John 10:10). Jesus took it for granted that men desire to save themselves and based his appeal on that assumption, asking, "What does it profit a man, to gain the whole world and forfeit his life? Or what shall a man give in return for his life?" (Mark 8:36).

My belief is that Jesus neither tried to repeal Nature's first law of self-preservation nor to demonstrate a dramatic exception to it. His purpose was to reveal the true way of understanding it.

Jesus interpreted "Nature's First Law" in the light of "Life's Deepest Law." Jesus taught that we must discover the real self which we are trying to save. If we are to see ourselves, we must look away from ourselves. If we would save ourselves, we must spend ourselves. We cannot hoard life as we can money. If we would develop ourselves, we must deny ourselves. He said: "If any man would come after me, let him deny himself and take up his cross and follow me. For whoever would save his life will lose it: and whoever loses his life for my sake and the gospel's will save it" (Mark 8:34-35).

While Jesus laid down so many laws for the wise use of the mind that he is rightly called the Master Teacher, nevertheless the supreme symbol of Christianity is not a book.

And while Jesus laid down so many principles of healing and laws of health for the body that he is rightly called the Great Physician, nevertheless the symbol of Christianity is not the caduceus, that emblem of the serpent coiled about the staff, which adorns the uniforms of the medical corps.

And while the birth of Christ at Bethlehem gives such a perennial glow to life that the story of Christmas never grows old, nevertheless the central symbol of Christianity is not a manger.

No, the supreme symbol of Christianity is the *cross*, because the deepest law of life is voluntary, redemptive suffering. St. Paul put it thus: "Bear one another's burdens, and so fulfil the law of Christ." That was the law of his life underlying all his other laws and all his works. Jesus, though sinless himself, went down to be baptized in the Jordan to show that he felt responsible for the sins of his society. He was the divine sin-bearer. Jesus, the strong young carpenter, who is never recorded as having been ill himself, so entered into the pains and sufferings of others that he felt them as his own. He was the divine pain-bearer. Jesus, the teacher whose talents might have won for him social prestige, threw in his lot with the poor and the oppressed. He was the divine poverty-bearer.

And if we would call ourselves Christians, whatever else we have or do not have, this one thing we must have, sufficient love to bear one another's burdens and so fulfill the law of Christ. I may have the virtues of purity and honesty and industry, but, if I have not love, they profit me nothing. I may have faith so that I can remove mountains of trouble and pray away all anxieties, but, if I have not love sufficient to help bear other's burdens, I am not fulfilling the law of Christ (cf. I Cor. 13).

Yes, the cross is the supreme symbol of Christianity because the deepest law of our Lord is voluntary, redemptive suffering. "Bear one another's burdens, and so fulfil the law of Christ" (Gal. 6:2).

Not by words, but by living, do we come to comprehend the cross. Yes, if we live long enough and suffer enough, the meaning of the cross grows clear. Henry Drummond was such a buoyant and vivacious personality that he was called "The Prince." He was a most popular preacher to students. He made religion so winsome that he won the young. But at the end he was laid low by long and agonizing pain. In his dying hours a friend played for him some of the hymns which had been popular in his services with students. Drummond listened in silence. Then the friend played and sang the old hymn with these lines:

> I'm not ashamed to own my Lord
> Or to defend His cause,
> Maintain the glory of His cross
> And honour all His laws.

Drummond's dying spirit was aroused. He marked time with his frail finger, joined in the words, and then said softly, "There is nothing to beat that." [65]

Yes, if we live long enough and suffer enough, that day comes when the vicarious love of the cross is not only the deepest law of life but also the dearest law of life.

Troubles We Can Avoid

Some of our troubles could be avoided by a better use of our intelligence. We drift into so many distressing difficulties through thoughtlessness and carelessness, through hasty judgment and foolish optimism, through lack of tact and limitation of knowledge.

When Jesus sent forth his disciples on a trial mission of teaching and healing, he said to them: "Be wise as serpents and innocent as doves" (Matt. 10:16). The Master Teacher would have his pupils use their wits to do their work in the right way and avoid unnecessary troubles. He bade his would-be followers to count the cost before they launched their undertakings lest they be like the man who started to build his house and was not able to finish.

Also, there are many troubles which can be avoided by a better use of the imagination. Some of our troubles exist only in our imagination. We may picture some person as hostile who bears us no ill will or may not even think about us at all. We may interpret some purely meaningless gesture as a slight. We may imagine some trouble for tomorrow which will not be there when the new day dawns. Thus we suffer unnecessarily through our self-centered sensitivity, we darken our days with the shadows of tomorrow, and sap our strength by self-inflicted wounds of worry.

Jesus would have us avoid the troubles that come through self-pity and self-centeredness and inflamed imagination. He said: "Do not be anxious about tomorrow, for tomorrow will be anxious for itself. Let the day's own trouble be sufficient for the day" (Matt. 6:34).

We might go on to quote many sayings of Jesus which would help toward peace of mind and freedom from unnecessary troubles by a better use of the imagination. And this is a phase of Christ's gospel which modern psychiatry and much popular preaching have been stressing.

Furthermore, in addition to the troubles we can avoid through better use of the intelligence and the imagination, there are those which we can escape through better use of the conscience. The Creator has endowed men with a conscience which serves as a warning against future troubles. In the immediacy of the moment the conscience may often seem a troublemaker. It prompts us to do unpleasant things. It may make us unpopular. It may deprive us of desired indulgences. But experience teaches us that the good things in life must be paid for in advance while the bad things in life are paid for afterwards. And obedience to conscience keeps us from those dismal and distressing installments of suffering for which we have to pay after our indulgences are over.

As a lad I was told that a cat's whiskers were its protection against getting into holes through which it could not pull its body safely. I am not sure of my biology at this point, but I am sure of my moral analogy. A person's conscience, like a cat's whiskers, is his protection against getting into situations which he cannot get out of safely.

The Scriptures make this crystal clear. "Do not be deceived; God is not mocked, for whatever a man sows, that he will also reap. . . . He who sows to his own flesh will from the flesh reap corruption; but he who sows to the Spirit will from the Spirit reap eternal life" (Gal. 6:7-8). Some years ago a man asked Dr. William E. Orchard, noted religious leader, whether or not the concept of hell could be dismissed in these days of modern enlightenment. With a strange quietness and a disturbing smile, Dr. Orchard replied, "I should not bank on it, if I were you."

Let us not make light of divine judgment. God is love. And to break the laws of love brings punishment. Not all prodigal sons are down and out. They may be quite up and in, and yet they may be feeding on the husks of life which will leave them hungry of heart. It is as true on Park Avenue as on the lanes of Galilee that, as Jesus said, "the gate is narrow and the way is hard, that leads to life, and those who find it are few" (Matt. 7:14).

But those who keep their consciences fit enough to guide them on the straight and narrow way will avoid the countless troubles which beset the sinner in this world and the next.

Troubles We Cannot Avoid

But however many troubles we can avoid by better use of our intelligence and imagination and conscience there are still some that remain. They may come from causes for which the individual is not responsible. Not by any means is all illness due to the fault of the sufferer nor is all unemployment due to laziness. Troubles may come from the presence of social evils in our community or from tornadoes and floods which hit our towns. So prevalent and unaccountable are misfortunes and disasters that Job's friend Eliphaz declared, "Man is born to trouble as the sparks fly upward" (Job 5:7).

And of these troubles, Paul says: "Each man will have to bear his own load" (Gal. 6:5). Each of us must carry his share of the world's burden just as each of us enjoys his share of the world's blessings. Just as each of us claims his inalienable right to life, liberty, and the pursuit of happiness—so each of us must assume his responsibility for life, liberty, and the pursuit of happiness. The early Christians recognized this individual responsibility. Recall the words: "If any would not work, neither should he eat" (II Thess. 10:3, K.J.V.). As I have heard, those were the scriptural words which Captain John Smith invoked at Jamestown to insure the stability of the new colony in Virginia. This emphasis on each one carrying his share of the social burden is the keystone of democracy and an essential in Christian discipleship.

To be sure, the individual can look around and say that the blessings and burdens of society are not equally borne. Perhaps you are familiar with the doggerel lines about how the rain falls upon both the just and unjust,

> But more upon the just because
> The unjust has the just's umbrella.[66]

We need governmental controls which will lessen the injustice of unequal sharing in life's loads, but we do not desire socialized or communized governmental systems which would take away individual initiative and responsibility. "Each man will have to bear his own load." There are some things no other person, no government can do for him.

In Thailand I heard of the difficulties of making democracy work. And I was reminded of the experience related some years ago by a Presbyterian missionary who was head of a boy's school in Thailand—or Siam, as we called it then. He developed athletics in the school curriculum. The native boys were eager to play soccer, but some of their parents could not quite grasp the players' point of view. One non-Christian parent, a wealthy Siamese, visited the school and said to the teacher: "I do not want my son to undergo the hardship of playing football. I have brought one of my servants with me. You must let my boy sit in a chair beside the playing field, and this servant will do the playing for him." It sounds funny, doesn't it? But therein lies a principle which some non-democratic societies failed to learn. There are some things which others cannot do for us however privileged our position. No one can eat for us. No one can sleep for us. No one can think for us. No one can grow for us. No one can bear for us what the Bible calls our "burden."

By that term the Bible means our wearing, daily tasks, the duties which weary us by their monotony or difficulty, the responsibilities which weigh upon us, the sorrows of loneliness, the bitterness of disappointment, the weakness of old age. "Every man (if he is manly) must bear his own load." Every person, if he is a Christian, must take his "share of suffering as a good soldier of Christ Jesus."

In these troubles which we cannot avoid, Christ can help us. He looked out upon his burdened countrymen and cried, "Come to me, all who labor and are heavy laden, and I will give you rest. Take my yoke upon you, and learn from me; for I am gentle and lowly in heart, and you will find rest for your souls. For my yoke is easy and my burden is light" (Matt. 11:28-30).

Christ does not exempt us from bearing our burdens, but he yokes himself with us in pulling our loads. He makes us feel that in enduring our drudgery and carrying our burdens we are workers together with God, that our tasks have meaning, that our efforts are going some place and getting somewhere, that our labor is not in vain in the Lord. Matthew Henry says Christ's yoke is easy because it is "lined with love."

Charles Dickens closes his *Tale of Two Cities* with a moving scene which James S. Stewart relates in the following passage:

The carts were rumbling through the thronged streets of Paris to the guillotine. In one of them there were two prisoners: a brave man who had once lost his soul but had found it again, and was now giving his life for his friend, and beside him a girl—little more than a child. She had seen him in the prison and had observed the gentleness and courage of his face. She said, "If I may ride with you, Citizen Evremonde, will you let me hold your hand? I am not afraid, but I am little and weak, and it will give me more courage." So when they rode together now, her hand was in his; and even when they reached the place of execution, there was no fear at all in her eyes. She looked at the quiet, composed face of the man beside her, and said, "I think you were sent to me by Heaven." [67]

In life there are some troubles we cannot avoid. "Each man shall have to bear his own load" (Gal. 6:5). But in bearing our loads no Christian is alone. He is yoked with Christ.

Troubles We Must Not Avoid

Having looked at the troubles we can avoid by better use of our intelligence, imagination and conscience, and having considered the troubles we cannot avoid, we are not true to Christ's teaching unless we heed a third counsel about burdens. In this same sixth chapter of Galatians, where each is bidden to bear his own burdens, we read this counsel, "Bear one another's burdens, and so fulfil the law of Christ" (Gal. 6:2).

The author uses two different Greek words for "burden" in these two passages. When he says, "Each man will have to bear his own burdens," he uses a Greek noun meaning "weight" or "assigned cargo" and the Revised Standard Version translates it "load." In his command, "Bear one another's burdens," the noun means "ship's cargo" or as some say, "supercargo." These two commands appearing in the same chapter imply that a follower of Christ must not only be manly enough to bear his own share of burdens, but he must help others in carrying the burdens too heavy for individual bearing.

Of course, we can avoid sharing the troubles of others. Thereby we would save ourselves much annoyance. At the age of 72 the late Charles M. Schwab, famous leader in the steel industry, became involved in a petty lawsuit, pressed by a young man whom he had tried to help. After he had finished his testimony, Mr. Schwab asked the indulgence of the court to make a statement to those present. He said that ninety per cent of his troubles had been the result of "being good to other people," and he advised young people to be hard-boiled and learn to say "no" if they wished to avoid the kind of unpleasantness he had frequently experienced. Then, with a smile lighting up his face, he added: "But you will have to do without friends, and you won't have much fun!"

And he might have added, "And you cannot call yourself a Christian." For Christ made it clear that only by bearing one another's burdens do we fulfill his law. He said: "If any man would come after me, let him deny himself and take up his cross and follow me."

And, in the New Testament, to take up one's cross means more than bearing one's own burdens. It means sharing some burden or rendering some service which we could refuse.

We are often confused at this point. A man once came to a minister and said: "I have my cross to bear. I have a nagging wife." Well, a nagging wife is a burden, to be sure, but to live with a troublesome wife or husband is not to take up one's cross, unless one goes beyond the line of duty in sacrifice and service.

You take up your cross when you go the second mile beyond the point where duty and decency compel you. You take up your cross when, for the sake of some high ideal, you endure suffering which could have been escaped by a lower standard. You take up your cross when you sacrifice your own comfort to serve the needs of your fellow men or risk unpopularity to fight for the rights of other races.

If you wish to see a man taking up his cross, look at David Livingstone. Familiar to us is the famous missionary going out from Scotland to bear the burdens of the African natives. But watch him a little more closely as he leads an expedition of natives across Africa through indescribable hardship until they finally reach a port city. When the port authorities recognized Livingstone they acclaimed him, for his reputation had risen high in England. They urged him to take a steamer then in harbor, and return to England where a tremendous welcome awaited him. But Livingstone replied that the men who had accompanied him would not then have the necessary leadership to bring them back safely to their homes. He had promised them if they would come with him, he would guide them home.

The authorities still pleaded, telling Livingstone that the natives would understand and find their way back. They told him that he had fever, that his body was wasted, that he would die if he went back. But Livingstone went back. And did die in the heart of Africa. He took up his cross.

The Spirit and Power of Compassion

Jesus bore his suffering with compassion for others. How plausibly he might have turned to other sufferers and said: "Why do you cry for your pains? Look how much greater mine are." But he never belittled the sufferings of others as we adults sometimes make light of the sorrows of little children. Mark Twain in his autobiography, told of his little daughter Susy, who at seven was breaking her heart over a broken toy and a picnic cancelled because of rain. Her mother told her not to cry over "little things." To this Susy responded: "Mamma, what is 'little things'?" We grownups forget that the loss of a little girl's doll, limp and ragged from much cuddling, and its rosy cheeks dirtied with much kissing, has power to bring heartbreak which the glib promises of a new doll tomorrow cannot quickly heal.

Jesus never belittled the heartbreaks of his hearers. He entered into their sufferings with compassion.

Read again in the New Testament how often the words come: "He was moved with compassion." He saw the multitude that they were like sheep without a shepherd, and "he was moved with compassion." He saw the people with their diseases and "he was moved with compassion," and he healed them. He saw them hungry and "he was moved with compassion," and he fed them.

Compassion is different from mercy. Mercy always carries an accent of judgment. We are merciful to those who perhaps deserve to be punished. Also compassion is different from pity. Pity carries the note of condescension. Oliver Goldsmith said you can never have pity between friends. To pity your friends destroys the necessary equality. But compassion is something without the taint of judgment that mercy possesses, something without the taint of condescension that pity possesses. Compassion is going out as an equal to share the feelings of the others.

Compassion does not flow like a stream from a higher to a lower level. Compassion moves as the tide moves across the ocean, that is, on the level drawn by the attraction of a power above.

Edward R. Murrow in *This I Believe* recounts the experience of a great American actress who lost her young daughter: "When my daughter died of polio, everybody stretched out a hand to help me, but at first I couldn't seem to bear the touch of anything, even the love of friends; no support seemed strong enough.

"While Mary was still sick, I used to go early in the morning to a little church near the hospital to pray. I had rather cut God out of my life, and I didn't have the nerve at the time to ask Him to make my daughter well—I only asked Him to help me understand. . . . I kept looking for a revelation, but nothing happened.

"And then, much later, I discovered that it had happened, right there in the church. I could recall, vividly, one by one, the people I had seen there. . . .

"Here was my revelation. Suddenly I realized that I was one of them. In my need I gained strength from the knowledge that they too had needs, and I felt an interdependence with them. . . . I experienced a flood of compassion for people. I was learning the meaning of 'Love thy neighbor.' " [68]

This suffering world today needs the rebirth of compassion. We of America are too inclined to think that we are showing mercy to people who are deserving of worse treatment. Or we may feel pity for the poverty of the less privileged, because we possess so much more. But it is compassion we need.

And with Christ's example of compassion before us, we cannot call ourselves his followers if our hearts do not go out to the world's sufferers. The church is reaching many through its medical, social, and educational missions, through hospitals and homes, through Church World Service and MCOR (Methodist Committee for

Overseas Relief), as well as through the General Board of Christian Social Concerns of The Methodist Church. The United Nations, also through such agencies as WHO (World Health Organization), UNICEF (which is now called the United Nations Children's Fund), and UNESCO (United Nations Educational, Scientific, and Cultural Organization)—is helping to feed the hungry and raise the physical, economic, and educational levels of needy adults and children through its emergency food and health programs and its agricultural, technical, and literacy projects. But we must give more and do more.

Stringfellow Barr, writing some years ago, cited figures which I cannot get out of my mind. He reminded us that 200,000 babies were born every day. (The number is 273,000* now.) "If you are born in the United States," he wrote 10 years ago"—and, remember, that's quite an *if* (one chance in 20)—you will probably live longer than a year. But if you are born in India, which is more likely, you have only a little better than a one-to-four chance of living more than a year. But cheer up! your chances in some places would be worse; and,

---

*"The total world population is approximately 2,900 million persons. This is the estimate of the United Nations Secretariat in its *Demographic Yearbook 1959* which reports on some 270 separate geographic areas of the world, . . .

". . . Some 100 million babies are born in the world each year. Total deaths amount to around 51 million.

"Africa has the highest estimated birth rate—45 per 1,000 population. Asia has an overall rate of 39 per 1,000. The region with the fastest rate of population increase is Middle America, where the relatively high birth—42 per 1,000—is combined with death rates which have been substantially lowered in recent years. The lowest continental birth rate is found in Europe—19 per 1,000—and within Europe the lowest regional rate—18 per 1,000—appears in the northern and western region. . . .

"The Yearbook lists mainland China, with an estimated 669 million inhabitants, as the country with the largest population. India follows with 403 million, the USSR with 209 million and the United States with 178 million. The four countries together total about 1,460 million and account for more than half of the world total. . . ." *United Nations Review*, "The News in Review," vol. 7, No. 4, October, 1960.

besides, even if you survive babyhood in India, you have only a fifty-fifty chance of growing to maturity."

In an age of rapid social change and population explosions, we must study the needs of the world and do more to improve community, national, and world conditions. We must actively support the work of the church and the United Nations with our informed opinion, our moral influence, our money, and our prayers. We still must feed the hungry, heal the sick, teach the illiterate, produce literature for new readers, and provide equal spiritual, social, and economic opportunities for people of all races.

The minimum requirement of a decent human being is that he should love those who love him. And from this minimum requisite Christ would have our love reach out to neighbors across the street, across the railroad tracks, across racial lines and through iron curtains. After World War I, the British novelist, A. S. M. Hutchinson, wrote a best selling book, *If Winter Comes*. The hero of the book, Mark Sabre, befriended an outcast girl whose lover was killed in the war before her baby was born out of wedlock. For his Good Samaritanism toward the poor girl, Mark Sabre was ostracized and persecuted. He expressed his motivation in these words: "Here was a human creature come to us. . . . Breathing the same air. . . . Sharing the same mortality. Responsible to the same God. . . . If you've got a grain, a jot of humanity, you must, you must, out of the very flesh and bones of you, respond to the cry of this your brother or your sister made as you, yourself, are made." [70]

To respond to the needs of a human being just because he or she is a human being—such is the breadth of Christ's love. But it seems a counsel of perfection utterly beyond us.

And it is, unless we get divine "booster power" to help us rise toward it. People on the street do not look lovable enough to arouse our affection. In these days of cold war, our hearts do not naturally warm up to our rivals. We must have a divine dynamic to help us.

And that is what Christ gives. After Judas left our Lord's Last Supper, Jesus turned to his disciples and said: "A new commandment I give to you, that you love one another: even as I have loved you, that you also love one another" (John 13:34). When Jesus cited his affection for his followers as the yardstick, he gave a new degree and a new dynamic of love. His was a love greater than enlightened self-interest, which prompts us to be friendly in order to be befriended, which prompts a strong nation to help a weaker nation in order to win friends and influence people against some rival power. Christ's was a love greater than the Golden Rule: "As you wish that men would do to you, do so to them" (Luke 6:31). When Christ said, "Love one another even as I have loved you," he was calling for love utterly selfless, free from all calculations of reciprocity.

The love we see there is more than a patriot dying for his country, more than a martyr dying for a cause, more than a friend dying for his friends. It is the love of God's Son who died for you and me.

> See, from His head, His hands, His feet,
>   Sorrow and love flow mingled down:
> Did e'er such love and sorrow meet,
>   Or thorns compose so rich a crown?
>
> Were the whole realm of nature mine,
>   That were an offering far too small;
> Love so amazing, so divine,
>   Demands my soul, my life, my all.[71]

NOTES

Chapter I Sources of Suffering

1. Sigmund Freud, *The Future of an Illusion*, quoted by Iago Galdston in an article entitled, "Job, Jung and Freud," in the *Bulletin of the New York Academy of Medicine*, Vol. 34, No. 12, December 1958, p. 776.
2. William Shakespeare, *King Lear*, Act I, Sc. 2, ll. 121-131.
3. Robert Louis Stevenson, "If This Were Faith," Stanza 3, in *A Treasury of Poems for Worship and Devotion*. Edited by Charles L. Wallis. (New York: Harper & Bros., 1959), p. 291.
4. C. S. Lewis, *The Problem of Pain* (New York: The Macmillan Co., 1944), pp. 1-2. (Used by permission)
5. Archibald MacLeish, *J. B.* (Boston: Houghton Mifflin Co., 1958).
6. C. S. Lewis, *The Problem of Pain*, p. 36.
7. William E. Henley, "Invictus."
8. William E. Henley, "In Memoriam Margaritae Sorori."

Chapter II The Pain of Living— How to Face it

9. Robert Burns, "To a Louse."
10. William Ernest Hocking, *Human Nature and Its Remaking* (New Haven: Yale University Press, rev. ed. 1923), p. 241.
11. James M. Barrie, *Courage* (New York: Chas. Scribner's Sons, 1922), pp. 22-23.
12. Rudyard Kipling, "If." Used by permission of Doubleday & Co.
13. Joshua Loth Liebman, *Peace of Mind* (New York: Simon & Schuster, 1946), pp. 82-83. (Used by permission)
14. Ernest M. Ligon, *The Psychology of Christian Personality* (New York: The Macmillan Co., 1935), p. 253.
15. Used by permission of Bishop F. Gerald Ensley.
16. James R. Blackwood, *The Soul of Frederick W. Robertson, The Brighton Preacher* (New York: Harper & Bros., 1947), p. 131.
17. Henry van Dyke, "The Prison and the Angel," in his *The Builders* (New York: Chas. Scribner's Sons, 1897).

Chapter III Physical and Mental Illness

18. C. S. Lewis, *The Problem of Pain*, p. 20.
19. Carl Michalson, *Faith for Personal Crises* (New York: Chas. Scribner's Sons, 1958), p. 138.
20. C. S. Lewis, *The Problem of Pain*, p. 104.
21. Quoted by William Adams Brown, in *Finding God in a New World* (New York: Harper & Bros., 1935), pp. 92-93.
22. Betsey Barton, *As Love Is Deep* (New York: Duell, Sloan & Pearce. Copyright 1957 by Betsey Barton), p. 65.
23. Quoted by Halford E. Luccock in *Preaching Values in The Epistles of Paul* (New York: Harper & Bros., 1959), Vol. I, p. 127.
24. Used by permission of the author.
25. James Payn, *The Backwater of Life* (Leipzig: Tauchnitz Edition, 1900), p. 51.
26. Quoted by Carl Michalson in *Faith for Personal Crises*, pp. 148-149.
27. John Ruskin, in *A Treasury of Comfort*, edited by Sidney Greenberg (New York: Crown Publishers, Inc., c. 1954), p. 111.
28. Robert D. Hershey, *Think About These Things* (Philadelphia: Muhlenberg Press, 1958), p. 160.
29. Used by permission of the writer.
30. Marietta Mansfield, Chaplain Intern in the Englewood Community Hospital, Englewood, N.J., March 15, 1959, under the auspices of The Council of Clinical Training for Pastoral Care and Counseling. Used by permission of the author.
31. J. D. Van Buskirk, *Religion, Healing and Health* (New York: The Macmillan Co., 1952), p. 74. Used with permission of The Macmillan Co.
32. Much of the material on pages 57-62 is from Wade H. Boggs, Jr., *Faith Healing and The Christian Faith* (Richmond, Va.; John Knox Press, 1956), pp. 56-73. Used by permission.

Chapter IV: Values of Suffering

33. Quoted by James S. Stewart in *The Strong Name* (New York: Chas. Scribner's Sons, 1951), pp. 150-151. See also Aldous Huxley, *Brave New World* (New York: Harper & Bros. Bantam Books, 1958), pp. 162-63.
34. Oliver Wendell Holmes, *The Poet at the Breakfast Table* (Boston: Houghton, Mifflin & Co., 1887), pp. 226-27.
35. Harry Lauder, in *A Treasury of Comfort*, ed. Sidney Greenberg (New York: Crown Publishers, Inc., c. 1954), p. 128.

36. For biographical data on Kagawa see *Toyohiko Kagawa, Japanese Prophet* . . . ed. by Jessie M. Trout. (N.Y.: Association Press, 1959), or Kagawa's *Songs from the Slums* (Nashville: Cokesbury Press, 1935), pp. 91-96.
37. Quoted in *The Ontario News,* January 14, 1959, p. 61. Copyright by the Christian Century Foundation, 1959. Reprinted by permission from *The Christian Century.*
38. Quoted by James S. Stewart, in *The Strong Name,* p. 152.
39. Leslie D. Weatherhead, *Why Do Men Suffer?* (New York: Abingdon-Cokesbury, 1936), p. 134.
40. Quoted by James S. Stewart in *The Strong Name,* p. 152.
41. Fanny and Robert Louis Stevenson, *Our Samoan Adventure* (New York: Harper & Bros., 1955), pp. 230-231.
42. Quoted by Carl Michalson, in *Faith for Personal Crises,* pp. 145-146.
(See also the *Teahouse of the August Moon,* a play by John Patrick, adapted from the novel by Vern Sneider (New York: G. P. Putnam, c. 1952), pp. 179-180.
43. Paul Tillich, *The Shaking of the Foundations* (New York: Chas. Scribner's Sons, 1950), pp. 52, 59.
44. Madame Chiang Kai-shek, *The Sure Victory* (Westwood, N.J.: Fleming H. Revell Co., 1955), pp. 17-19.
45. Source unknown.
46. Oscar Fisher Blackwelder, Exposition, "The Epistle to the Galatians," in *The Interpreter's Bible* (New York: Abingdon Press, 1953), Vol. 10, p. 575.
47. Quoted in *The Meaning of the Cross* by Henry Sloane Coffin (New York: Chas. Scribner's Sons, 1931), pp. 138-139.
48. Ralph Waldo Emerson, "Abraham Lincoln," in *The Writings of Emerson* (New York: Random House, 1950), p. 918.

Chapter V: Death

49. William Cullen Bryant, "To a Waterfowl," stanza 8, in *A Treasury of Comfort,* ed. Sidney Greenberg (New York: Crown Publishers, Inc., 1954), p. 94.
50. Quoted by Carl Michalson in *Faith for Personal Crises,* pp. 167-168.
51. Carl Michalson, *Faith for Personal Crises,* pp. 174-175.
52. John Baillie, *And the Life Everlasting* (New York: Chas. Scribner's Sons, 1933), pp. 237-238.
53. John Greenleaf Whittier, in *The Methodist Hymnal* (Nashville: The Methodist Publishing House, 1939), Hymn No. 517. From "The Eternal Goodness," in *Whittier's Complete Poems.* c. 1894, Houghton Mifflin Co.

54. Douglas V. Steere, *On Beginning From Within* (New York: Harper & Bros., 1943), Chapter V, pp. 132-133.
55. John Fawcett, in *The Methodist Hymnal*, Hymn No. 416.
56. Carl Michalson, *Faith for Personal Crises*, p. 160.
57. W. R. Inge, *Personal Religion and the Life of Devotion* (London: Longmans, Green & Co., 1927), pp. 89-90. Used by permission.
58. William Allen White, in *A Treasury of Comfort*, ed. Sidney Greenberg, p. 89. Quoted from *The El Dorado Times*, January 1952.
59. Betsey Barton. *As Love Is Deep*, p. 51.
60. Ralph Waldo Emerson, "Threnody" in, *The Writings of Emerson* (New York: Random House, 1950), p. 782.
61. Robert F. Horton, *Oliver Cromwell, A Study in Personal Religion* (New York: Thos. Whittaker, 1897), pp. 202-204.
62. Frederick William Faber, in *The Methodist Hymnal*, Hymn No. 76.
63. William Shakespeare, *Henry VIII*, Act III, Sc. 2, ll. 456-458.

Chapter VI: Fellowship of Suffering

64. J. H. Denison, *Mark Hopkins*, A Biography (New York: Chas. Scribner's Sons, 1935), p. 237.
65. George Adam Smith, *The Life of Henry Drummond* (New York: Doubleday & McClure, Co., 1898), p. 502.
66. Robert Hershey, *Think About These Things*, p. 164.
67. Quoted by James S. Stewart in *The Strong Name*, p. 164. See also Charles Dickens, *A Tale of Two Cities* (New York: The New American Library, 1960), pp. 357, 375.
68. Helen Hayes, "A Morning Prayer in a Little Church," from *This I Believe*, Edward R. Murrow, ed. (New York: Simon & Schuster), pp. 65-66. (Copyright 1952 by Help, Inc. Used by permission of Simon & Schuster.)
69. Stringfellow Barr, *Let's Join the Human Race* (Chicago: University of Chicago Press, 1950), pp. 2-3.
70. A. S. M. Hutchinson, *If Winter Comes* (Boston: Little, Brown & Co., 1923), p. 343.
71. Isaac Watts, in *The Methodist Hymnal*, Hymn No. 148.

BIBLIOGRAPHY

BOOKS RELATED TO THE PROBLEM OF SUFFERING

The books listed below may be borrowed from your public, college, or pastor's libraries. Those in print may be ordered from the Cokesbury Bookstore serving your territory. Prices are subject to change.

GUIDE TO THE MEANING OF SUFFERING. Leila Bagley Rumble. 35 cents. Order from Literature Headquarters, 7820 Reading Road, Cincinnati 37, Ohio.

THE MEANING OF THE CROSS. Henry Sloane Coffin. New York: Chas. Scribner's Sons, 1959. $2.50.

MEET JOE ROSS. Russell L. Dicks, Nashville: Abingdon Press, 1957. $2.50.

STUMBLING BLOCK—Alcohol and Christian Responsibility. Douglas Jackson. 1960. (Order from Literature Headquarters, 7820 Reading Road, Cincinnati 37, Ohio.) 75 cents.

THE PROBLEM OF PAIN. C. S. Lewis. New York: The Macmillan Co., 1943. $3.50.

FAITH FOR PERSONAL CRISES. Carl Michalson. New York: Chas. Scribner's Sons, 1958. $3.50.

THE REVELATION OF GOD IN HUMAN SUFFERING. Wayne E. Oates. Philadelphia: Westminster Press, 1959. $2.75.

GOD OUR CONTEMPORARY. J. B. Phillips. New York: The Macmillan Co., 1960. $2.50. Paper, $1.25.

WHEN TROUBLE COMES. James E. Sellers. Nashville: Abingdon Press, 1960. $2.00.

PSYCHOLOGY, RELIGION, AND HEALING. Leslie D. Weatherhead. Nashville: Abingdon Press, 1952. $5.00. Paper (Apex), 1959. $1.75.

THE WILL OF GOD. Leslie D. Weatherhead. Nashville: Abingdon Press, 1945. Paper, 50 cents. (Available from Literature Headquarters.)

THE PROBLEM OF EVIL. J. S. WHALE. New York: The Macmillan Co. (Viewpoint No. 5), 1949. 63 pages. 60 cents.

BOOKS FOR FURTHER READING*

THE LITERATURE OF THE OLD TESTAMENT. Julius A. Bewer. New York: Columbia University Press. Rev. ed., 1933. $4.50. (Chapters 7, 11, 14, 19.)

---

* For a list of related booklets and audio-visuals, see *Guide* to *The Meaning of Suffering* by Leila Bagley Rumble. (Available from Literature Headquarters, 7820 Reading Road, Cincinnati 37, Ohio.) 35 cents.

DEVOTIONAL INTRODUCTION TO JOB. Andrew W. Blackwood, Jr. Grand Rapids, Michigan: Baker Book House, 1959. $2.95.

FAITH HEALING AND THE CHRISTIAN FAITH. Wade H. Boggs, Jr. Richmond: John Knox Press, 1956. $3.50.

TRAGIC THEMES IN WESTERN LITERATURE. Cleanth Brooks, ed. New Haven: Yale University Press, 1960. Paper, $1.25.

TOWARD HEALTH AND WHOLENESS. Russell L. Dicks. New York: The Macmillan Co., 1960. $3.50.

HEALING: HUMAN AND DIVINE. Simon Doninger, ed. New York: Association Press, 1957. $3.50.

MIND AND BODY: PSYCHOSOMATIC MEDICINE. Flanders Dunbar. New York: Random House, Inc., Revised edition, 1955. $3.50.

GUIDE TO UNDERSTANDING THE BIBLE. Harry Emerson Fosdick. New York: Harper & Bros., 1938. $5.00. (Torchbooks, 1956. Paper, $1.75) Chapter 4 (pp. 152-200).

THE ONLY WAR WE SEEK—(against poverty, disease, hunger and illiteracy). Arthur Goodfriend. With a foreword by Chester Bowles. A Pictorial. New York: Farrar, Straus and Young. 1951. $3.00.

ON GROWING OLD. Sibyl Harton. New York: Morehouse-Gorham, 1958. $2.50.

UNDERSTANDING GRIEF. Edgar N. Jackson. Nashville: Abingdon Press, 1957. $3.50.

PSYCHOLOGY OF RELIGION. Paul E. Johnson. Nashville: Abingdon Press, rev. ed., 1959. $5.00.

CHRIST AND HUMAN SUFFERING. E. Stanley Jones, Nashville: Abingdon Press, c. 1933. $2.00.

VICTORIOUS LIVING. E. Stanley Jones. Nashville: Abingdon Press, 1936. $3.00.

SONGS FROM THE SLUMS. Toyohiko Kagawa. Nashville: Abingdon Press, 1935. $1.50.

FEAR AND TREMBLING and THE SICKNESS UNTO DEATH. Soren Kierkegaard. Garden City, N.Y.: Anchor Books, 1954. 95 cents.

CHRIST AND THE HOPE OF GLORY. John Knox. Nashville: Abingdon Press, 1960. $1.00.

THE DEATH OF CHRIST. John Knox. Nashville: Abingdon Press, 1958. $2.75.

THE MINISTRY OF HEALING. John Ellis Large. New York: Morehouse-Gorham, 1959. $3.00.

LOVE AGAINST HATE. Karl A. Menninger, with collaboration of Jeanetta L. Menninger. New York: Harcourt, Brace & Co., 1959. $4.75. Harvest Book (HB28) Paper, $1.95.

A GENUINELY HUMAN EXISTENCE—TOWARDS A CHRISTIAN PSYCHOLOGY. Stephen C. Neill. Garden City, N.Y.: Doubleday & Co., 1959. $4.50.

BEYOND TRAGEDY. Reinhold Niebuhr. New York: Chas. Scribner's Sons, 1938. $3.95.

THE TRAGIC VISION AND THE CHRISTIAN FAITH. Nathan A. Scott, Jr., ed. New York: Association Press, 1957. $4.50.

THE SHAKING OF THE FOUNDATIONS. Paul Tillich. New York: Chas. Scribner's Sons, 1948. $2.95.

WHY DO MEN SUFFER? Leslie D. Weatherhead. Nashville: Abingdon Press. 1960 (Apex). $1.25.

VICTOR AND VICTIM: THE CHRISTIAN DOCTRINE OF REDEMPTION. J. S. Whale. New York: Cambridge University Press, 1960. $2.95.

THE DARK ROAD TO TRIUMPH. Clayton E. Williams. New York: Crowell Publishing Co., 1960. $2.75.

THE HEALINGS OF THE BIBLE. Nellie B. Woods, ed. New York: Hawthorn Books, Inc., 1958. $1.00.

SPIRITUAL THERAPY. Richard K. Young and Albert L. Meiburg. New York: Harper & Bros., 1960. $3.50.

SYMBOLISM OF THE COVER

Each person looking at the cover of this book may interpret its meaning differently, coloring its symbolism with the darker hues of his own suffering and with the brighter light of hope and spiritual renewal.

The symbols suggested by the artist include the dark rocky precipice indicating dangers and hardship, physical and mental distress, unexplained tragedy and loss.

The shaft of bright light, streaming down into the deep crevice, may suggest the grace and mercy of God reaching into the dark depths of man's doubt, despair, and pain. The single white flower nourished by the ray of heavenly light may suggest new life made possible by the light of God—in the midst of suffering and desolation. The small cross surmounting the flower may symbolize resurrection, the result of crucifixion, rebirth, and triumph over evil and death; renewal and the promise of life reborn into gladness—even in the midst of darkness.

Woman's Division of Christian Service
Board of Missions, The Methodist Church
Literature Headquarters
7820 Reading Road, Cincinnati 37, Ohio
Price, 75 cents